BOX CAR

BOX CAR

By

George H. Weber

1stBooks-rev.06/29/00

ABOUT THE BOOK

Written in the spirit of *Huckleberry Finn* and *Tom Sawyer*—not on a Mississippi River raft, but on the railroads and highways of South Dakota—this book captures the hopes, aspirations and excitement-seeking of two South Dakota adolescent boys.

Share the high adventure of Carl and Wes as they ride the freights and hitchhike across South Dakota and back, seeing the wonders of the Bad Lands, Mt. Rushmore and the Black Hills, all on a shoestring budget. Meet their generous benefactors who help them along the way, many of whom are regular folks. Others are distinctive, colorful characters. Enjoy the scenery—the exotic color and strangeness of the Bad Lands, the penetrating force of Mt. Rushmore and the dark mystery of the Black Hills. Laugh at Carl and Wes as they explore the excitement of a casino and the secrets of a bordello. Cringe as they cope with the dangers of freight trains and fight against continued incarceration by a local police chief interested in furthering his political career. Grieve as they are locked in a box car and left on an isolated railroad siding. Finally, rejoice as they make their final part of their journey home sitting inside a passenger train.

ACKNOWLEDGMENTS

My appreciation extends to several sources. First, my family and friends who have listened patiently and with interest to my many tellings of this story. Members of the Sun City Center Writers' Club critiqued aspects of the manuscript, and the club's president, Don Looper, an achieved author, gave a written commentary of unusual insight. Susan P. Fossett, a 'word-processor' of great skill, has also been a keen editorial consultant and advisor. Many Ann Llewelyn has been a constant 'critical ear' and has shared her observations of the manuscript. My thanks to all of these people.

DEDICATION

This book is dedicated to my lifelong friend and fellow high school adventurer, Dr. Walter Zeeb. I hope that Walt's indomitable sense of humor will not be blunted by my fictionalizing parts of our exciting, though somewhat reckless, travel. Had it not been his dauntless courage and good spirits, we might not have completed our journey.

TABLE OF CONTENTS

Forthcoming from George H. Weber

Novels
Unsettled Libido

Short Stories
In Pursuit of Altruism

Non-fiction
Eldercare: A Clinical Primer for Volunteers

AUTHOR' S FOREWORD

The reader may legitimately ask, "Is *Box Car* fiction or nonfiction?" The answer is, both. With the exception of "Shy Anne's Rooms" and "Traveling and Criminal Justice," the book is autobiographical and nonfiction. The 1937 events and conversations are recollected at several stages later in life; consequently, some details have blurred and been modified by memory. However, the recalled themes clearly capture the significant happenings, emotions and activities of an adventuresome trip across South Dakota and back, planned spontaneously by a couple of devil-may-care adolescents—my good friend Wes and myself.

The book tells of Wes's and my search for a broader horizon and personal fulfillment, and captures our imagination, ingenuity, determination and our dedicated but unspoken relationship.

The freight train-riding, box car episode, hitchhiking and general sightseeing did not match the awesome beauty of Mt. Rushmore, the Black Hills and the Badlands; nevertheless, they generated joy, fear, panic and desperation along with exhilarating excitement, almost beyond our capacity to manage.

As a matter of principle, I changed the names of persons and places, including those persons we met during our journey, and in one instance, Silverthorne, the town in which we were served criminal justice.

Hopefully the reader will see the book as an odyssey of adolescent human spirit as it expressed itself.

Chapter 1
Days of Planning

Wes and I sat on a creek bank fishing one August afternoon in 1937. Though ninety degrees, it was pleasant in the shade of large elm trees and a cool breeze. The fish weren't biting so we idled our time away, leisurely puffing on Luckies taken from the cab of Wes's father's truck. We handled the cigarettes as we had seen Humphry Bogart do in the movies. However, we squinted and our eyes watered from the smoke as it curled skyward, and we coughed frequently.

Wes and I were best of friends, having known each other since the first grade, where both of us played in the toy band and learned how to read and color original designs. The succeeding years of grade school helped us do ever more complicated arithmetic, read ever more complex literature and play ever more energetic sports. Now, we were about to enter our junior year in high school and hoped to make the football team. Our immediate focus, however, was summer vacation, and we talked about the highlights thus far: for example, having been warned by the game warden, "Stop swimming in the fish hatchery or I'll turn you over to the police!"; having been threatened by a truck gardener, "Stay out of my watermelon patch or I'll shoot you!"; having been informed by the night cop, "I don't know who has been knocking out these street lights, but if it's either of you, you better stop or I'll take you to court!"; and being warned by a neighbor to stop shooting pigeons off his shed, "One more time and it will go hard with you two."

The smoke was too much for us and tears rolled down our cheeks. Wes wiped his away with the back of his shirt sleeve and I did the same. An exceptionally serious expression covered his narrow, handsome face, unlike the glee he showed in describing the warnings of the game warden, the truck gardener and the police. He spoke of a different topic.

"It's a damned shame we've never been to the Black Hills. People come from all over the country to see them, and we live right here in the state and have never seen them. What's worse, a lot of people right here in town have been there too. But where have we been? No place. We live in this little town of eight hundred people, have never been any place, never seen anything excepting what's in the movies."

I picked up his lament. "Or what other people, like teachers, tell us, and what we read. But we haven't been any place but Yankton, and that's not much. Haven't even been over to Nebraska."

Wes hadn't explained why we hadn't been to the Black Hills or anywhere else. It was too embarrassing to acknowledge. Our families were too poor to take us. I appreciated his skipping the poverty thing, looked to the ground and said nothing.

Provoked by his lament, I asked, "Doesn't your Dad know some truckers who make that run? You know, like every other week."

Wes shook his head. "His run doesn't go that way. We need to go north about fifty miles to Mitchell and then two to three hundred miles west. He goes the opposite direction. But just to be sure, I'll ask him."

Having exhausted our ideas, we stubbed out our cigarettes, pulled our fishing lines out of the water and walked home. We were content but determined.

The following day saw us at the same spot, lighting up and throwing our lines into the water. Wes glumly reported, "He doesn't know anybody who makes the Black Hills run. Nobody."

"Too bad. Maybe we can hitchhike it."

"Nobody will pick us up. Not a couple of young kids. Not after the kidnaping murder by a hitchhiker last month. Everybody is scared. We'd be there on the road forever."

I shrugged and Wes continued, "Besides, your sister and my parents wouldn't okay a hitchhiking trip. They'll be afraid for our safety."

"We don't have to tell them," I argued, and repeated, "We don't have to tell them."

The reasoning moved back and forth between us, resulting in a strategy in which Wes would tell his parents that we have a ride to the Hills with relatives of mine and I would tell my sister we have a ride with a trucker, an acquaintance of Wes's father. As our families didn't know each other well, we believed they wouldn't discuss our planned adventure. They didn't.

Once we decided to go, we confronted our meager budget, lack of provisions, poor prospects for shelter and no transportation. Moreover, we needed to tie down exactly where we wanted to go. Yet we were determined to go, thinking that any details could be surmounted.

We became the busiest adolescents in Sioux Center during the following two weeks—mowing lawns, chopping weeds, cleaning basements and garages, all to improve our budgets. In spite of our hard work, we earned only $5.50 each, bringing our individual purses to $17.50.

"Geez, is that all we made?" Wes complained.

"That's it," I affirmed. "If you don't think it's enough we can try to find other jobs, but I think we've done about all there is to do in Sioux Center, and if we wait we'll never make the trip. At least not this summer. We're into August now, August third. Football practice starts the twenty-seventh. It's either now or next year."

"I think we better go now. We'll make the money do somehow," Wes reasoned.

I nodded.

We borrowed a pup tent from our friend Clarence. It was a strange shelter, a relic of World War I. It was divided into two halves. Buttons and their corresponding holes ran across the tops, which facilitated putting the two halves together. Each soldier had carried a "shelter half." They would buddy up with each other and have a tent. With the exception of the Evans Athletic dorm in Rapid City, the tent was our only assured shelter. The dorm was a contribution to the State School of Mines Athletic Department from Mr. Evans, a local businessman, and was located in the large basement of his service station. Athletes lived free of charge in exchange for their athletic skills. My brother had stayed there the previous school year, so we felt optimistic about gaining access.

Wes complained, "That damned tent is a relic, especially with those buttons running across the top. I hope it keeps the rain out. I don't think it'll do it."

"The way the two halves double over should take care of any rain," I assured. "We'll be okay. Don't worry."

Wes was not satisfied, however. "And it doesn't have a door on it. There should be a flap of canvas for that. The wind will blow in, and animals will come in."

Again, I assured, "We'll be okay. Anyway, it's all we have. Besides, Clarence said what he gave us is the whole thing. We can pin a blanket on each shelter half. That's to ease the carrying. Then we'll have something to keep us warm. You know, we'll unpin them at night and pull them over us."

We pilfered food from our pantries, and in the instance of Wes, also from his basement. His father bought cases of food from wholesale houses on his trucking runs and lined them up in the basement, so Wes's contribution was beyond mine. Cans of beans, spaghetti, corn and peaches were fitted into two suitcases, along with a change of clothes, some extra underwear and sox. A couple of loaves of bread were stuffed in as well. We felt good about that part of our preparation. As an afterthought we added jackets to our suitcases, as we heard the nights were cold in the Black Hills. Somehow the suitcases accommodated them.

"This stuff is heavy," Wes groaned as he lifted his luggage. "Really heavy!"

"Get us into shape for football, especially if we carry them around for a couple of weeks," I replied.

"That's one way of looking at it," Wes laughed, and I nodded.

The attendant at the local Texaco station gave us a road map of South Dakota and we concentrated on our general route, points of interest and public campgrounds. Indeed, we turned our dreams of going West into concrete planning. I swore we could see the Black Hills in a week at the most. Our time was getting short.

We pored over the map and saw the route was quite simple: fifty miles north to Mitchell; three hundred and twenty miles west to Rapid City; fifty miles south to Hot Springs, including stops at the Rushmore Memorial and related sights; one hundred miles north to Sturgis, Lead and Deadwood; fifty miles back to Rapid City; and then return to Mitchell and Sioux Center. The Bad Lands, Rushmore Memorial, Wind Cave, Deadwood's Boot Hill Cemetery and the Corn Palace were among our listed places to see. Many towns along the way were new to us, and that added to the excitement. We had never heard of Presho, Murdo, Kadoka and others. They were west of the Missouri River that ran across the middle of the state—a section of the state that was new to us. We had been out of Sioux Center, but not far. We noted the campgrounds along the way and marked them on the map.

Instructed by the map, we felt in control of things. Yet we had not decided on our mode of travel. Would it be hitchhiking, or freight train riding, or some combination of the two? Or might some unidentified source—like a relative or a friend—be going to Rapid City? However, we had already ruled that out. We discussed the matter in detail and argued some.

I reasoned, "I don't want to be standing on Highway 35 at the north end of town thumbing a ride but not getting one. People will see us, and sure as hell will tell your folks and my sister. That will bring our lie about having an assured ride into the open. We can't stand that. You know people from here don't go anyplace, and people traveling through are very scarce. There's no chance for a ride."

Wes picked up, "I know, but I'm not for wrestling a freight. Too many problems. Too dangerous. We've had a lot of fun catching them out of town a ways and riding them in. But they are dangerous!"

"We'll take care, be careful, and we should be okay," I argued.

"I'll do it, but I really don't like it. But yes, I'll do it."

"Wes, I know it will be okay." I was pleased that Wes agreed. That was essential to making this trip successful. We had been friends for a long time and our communication, while often short, was good.

We decided to catch a five o'clock a.m. freight train. It would deliver us to Mitchell in about two hours. Mitchell, a town of about eight thousand people, was fifty miles north of Sioux Center. That timing would give us an early start, and out of view of the people in the community. We knew the movement of freight trains as a matter of small town information.

However, our first-hand experience reached beyond that. We had walked the tracks south of town for about a mile on a number of occasions. It was a good spot because the engine had to slow to accommodate a bend and in anticipation of stopping for water in Sioux Center. One following the other, Wes and I had run along the side of the freight cars, disregarding the unevenness of the road bed, punctuated by railroad ties and crushed rock. When we were in rhythm with the train we extended ourselves upwards, grabbed the ladder of a car and jumped upwards. The thrust of the car's forward motion was violent, catching us and slamming us up against its side. Though the impact was intense, we placed our feet on a low rung of the ladder and crawled to the top of the car. Exhilarated, we rode on the top until we reached the water tower, at which point we climbed down and jumped off. We were aware of the danger. We could turn an ankle on the uneven surface and fall onto the tracks, or fail to gain a firm grasp on the ladder and be swept under one of the wheels. However, the excitement of the activity and a devil-may-care attitude propelled us on. This attitude, along with hyper enthusiasm for sightseeing, readied us for our coming adventures.

Chapter Two
Day One: Modes of Travel

My home was about a half mile from the railroad yard and its water tower, closer than Wes's place. So we chose it as the place to sleep our last night before the eventful morning. I set the alarm clock for four a.m. That, however, wasn't necessary, as the excitement constantly interrupted our sleep. We were up before four, turned off the alarm, dressed and crept downstairs, had a hasty breakfast and left the house, each carrying a suitcase and one half of the pup tent. We had not awakened my sister or her husband so we didn't have to give any final explanations. We were on our way.

It was dark, cool and damp, so different from the daytime. During the short walk to the railroad depot, occasional crickets chirped and let us know we were not alone. That and an occasional dog barking in the distance sharpened our already overly alert senses as we entered the railroad yard.

Tensed by the situation, especially the unknowns ahead, I turned to Wes and spoke for the first time since leaving the house. There we had spoken only in brief exchanges and gestures and grunts. Those brief expressions included, "It's time to get up," "Let's go downstairs," "Here's the cereal," and, "I think we're ready to go." Now I leaned close to Wes as we walked and said, mainly to reassure myself, "I think we're on time."

Wes nodded and I added, "I think we'll be okay."

And Wes nodded again. He looked at his wrist watch and corrected, "We're a half hour early."

"I know. I know," I defended, "but we have to figure out just how we're going to climb aboard, and onto what."

Three tall grain elevators bordered the tracks and stood like huge giants guarding a hallowed place. We hurried to their protection, surveying the depot about fifty yards ahead. We were shocked to see Shorty Hertz, the night cop, on the dimly lit platform outside the depot. He paced back and forth like a prison guard watching a group of inmates.

Wes exclaimed quietly, but the full force of his concern was clear. "Damn it! That guy always gives us trouble even when he doesn't try. Just being there on the platform is bad—bad for us."

I whispered, "We've got to keep out of his sight by all means. We can't let him see us."

Wes nodded and with that I pointed across the tracks. When Shorty turned his back we scampered across to a ditch on the other side. It hid us well, but we were driven out of there by swarming mosquitos. We ran to a small clump of trees just a short distance ahead as Shorty Hertz continued to face the other direction.

Our quick maneuvers and the tenseness of the situation caused us to laugh and laugh. We covered our mouths to mute the noise and luckily remained out of Shorty's scope. This was one of our continuing encounters with him. The one that had irritated him the most was, on the previous Halloween we tipped his outhouse over while he was busy in another part of town. He wasn't sure it was us, but he was clearly suspicious. We were only sorry he hadn't been in it when it toppled over.

We felt safe among the trees and waited. However, our tension did not drop and I felt my heart beat on the inside of my chest wall. At exactly five o'clock a.m. the train slowed as it came around the familiar bend south of town. It whistled at the crossroads immediately out of town and continued toward us. Its exceptionally bright headlight lit the whole area. We worried that it would expose us to Shorty. However, such did not happen and the train whizzed by and began braking to stop by the water tower. Hissing steam and screeching brakes and a unique kind of puffing flowed from the engine. It was awesome and we shrunk among the trees until the engine came to a complete halt. It then went into a strange type of breathing and puffing. We had heard it many times before, but this morning it breathed more excitement into us than we could comfortably stand.

"Let's go," I exclaimed, yet keeping my voice down.

We burst from our hiding place holding the luggage closely at our sides. We ran back and forth by the train, searching for an open box car. None, however, was to be found. There were other kinds of cars—petroleum cars, sand cars, cattle cars—but no open box cars. We tried in vain to open several box cars, only to find them sealed. We weren't law abiding teenagers, but we were not about to break a sealed railroad car door. In the meantime the engine had its fill of water and the engineer blew its whistle. At the same time the brakeman at the end of the train waved his lantern. Our tension reached a new high, as we didn't have a car to ride in and the train was about to leave.

I pointed to the top of a nearby boxcar and called out, "Up there!" We had done such riding on occasions when we caught freight trains south of town and rode them to the water tank, all for fun. In addition, we had seen hoboes do it many times. Wes thought a few seconds and shouted, "No. . . . Not up there!" We had seen hundreds of men riding on top of box cars, even sleeping up there. They were all kinds of men out of work going from one place to another in search of jobs. Of course, some bums just wandering around were included in these riders. But whatever the character of these riders, we agreed the top of a box car was not for us.

The engineer blew the whistle the third and final time. There was no alternative to the petroleum car immediately before us. It was familiar to us, but in all of our experimenting with riding freight cars we had never boarded one of those before. They were too dangerous. There was only a catwalk on each side of the huge tank, and the wheels of the car were alarmingly close to the catwalk. We glanced at each other for just a moment and intuitively decided that the petroleum car was our only chance. We threw our baggage on the catwalk and climbed on ourselves. I remained up front on the left side of the car, but since there was room for only one there, Wes stepped over the clasp that connected the car to the one ahead of it, and pulled his luggage with him and seated himself on the right side. Though dangerous because of the uncertain footing and open spaces from the left to the right side of the car, he made it okay, put his stuff down, laughed and waved.

I was nervous and excited, and I laughed too.

The design of the petroleum car, though large, was simple. The steel tank was cylindrical and held several thousand gallons of petroleum. It was framed by a rectangular enclosure that rested on coiled springs. They were attached to the axles. Four steel wheels were mounted on them and had contact with the rails. A wooden catwalk was mounted on each side of the tank about a foot above the wheels. That would be our headquarters for the next couple of hours.

We had just placed the shelter halves behind us and the suitcases ahead of us when the train violently jerked back to insure that all the clasps linking the cars together were fastened, and then almost as suddenly jerked ahead. We were shocked by the violence of the movements. We gripped the sides of the catwalk tightly, as there were no handles or guard rails to hang onto. I had difficulty breathing. The knuckles on our hands turned white. Our precarious positions and the sweat on my hands made it a dangerous situation. I felt like I was sitting on a volcano. Not only in anguish over myself and Wes, I worried about our shelter halves and luggage, and I momentarily wished we had chosen hitchhiking instead of riding the freight.

I held on with all my might as the freight pulled out of town and built up its speed. However, once it gained its traveling speed, I relaxed. My initial panic dropped to a watchful awareness. What had been a dangerous situation became an exciting routine.

I looked over at Wes to see how he was doing. He saw my scared expression and yelled, "Ride 'em, cowboy!" I joined him in laughter and gave Shorty Hertz a thought, mainly that we had outsmarted him again. In my glee I was sorry we hadn't passed by the station platform in riding out of town, as we could have waved, in a sense tweaking his nose, but our petroleum car was lined up beyond the platform when we boarded and he was out of view. Our usual devil-may-care attitude was back with us.

It was almost fully light now, as about twenty minutes had sped by after the train had pulled out of Sioux Center. The engine raced on and we clearly saw its hugeness, blackness and felt its awesome power when it rounded a bend. Having adapted to our situation we viewed the flat countryside marked with tracts of golden grain ready for harvest, green pastures and fields of corn. Periodic groves of cottonwood trees were crowded into the landscape, especially around the farm homes and outbuildings. Each farm had a towering windmill that gave it a distinctive look. We saw farmers bring cows into their farmyards for milking, and as we traveled further we saw other farmers turn their cows out to pasture after they had been milked. Still other farmers fed their hogs, calves and chickens. Following this, we saw farmers go into their fields, either to harvest grain or cultivate corn.

The small farms raised oats, wheat, barley and corn along with cattle, hogs and chickens. All of this unfolded before us as we rode through Bon Homme, Hutchinson and Madison counties. The towns of Kaylor, Tripp, Parkston, and Woonsocket stood out along the way—all thriving, small trading and service centers for the farms about them. In addition to their level of income, they sought eminence through high school sports, city baseball, pheasant hunting, Fourth of July celebrations, church socials, presence of a swimming pool and Saturday night performance by a city band.

We were part of such community life in Sioux Center and felt it keenly. We were very proud of our city baseball team and its wins over surrounding town teams. It gave us a sense of superiority, a feeling of winners, of dominance. We also were proud of our high school athletic teams, especially basketball and football, and their win and loss records. We identified ourselves with the outstanding players and hoped we would follow in their footsteps. Since we planned to make the football team in several weeks, that pride was very much with us.

The clickety-clacking of the railroad car wheels on the breaks in the tracks gave the ride a steady rhythm and regularity. A cool, clean air blew around our faces and bodies and added to the pleasure of the ride. But the direction of the wind suddenly shifted and showered us with sparks and soot, burning our faces and necks and our hands and arms, any area not covered with clothing. Wes and I looked at each other, screaming in pain but unable to help ourselves or each other. In panic, and jeopardizing our safety, we unfurled the shelter halves and buried ourselves

11

under them. We struggled to maintain ourselves and the suitcases on the catwalk. In doing so we drove our fingernails into wood of the catwalk and pressed our heads on the suitcases to hold them in place. I heard Wes call, though it was muffled coming through the shelter half, "Hold on, for God's sake. Hold on." I made that out of his calling.

I knew his situation was as precarious as mine and I called back, "You too, You too!"

My fear catapulted to a still higher level as my buttocks began to slide off the catwalk, and I pulled desperately to right myself. I could hear the clicketing of the wheels on the tracks more loudly than ever before, and as I looked down I could see the railroad ties flying by the wheels. With my hands pulling on the opposite side of the catwalk and my fingernails driven into its wood I was holding my slide, but no more than that. Without planning I called aloud, "Oh, God, save me! Save me!"

I continued to struggle and I heard Wes shout, "Hold on! Hold on!"

I pulled with all my might, quite uncertain about my whereabouts because of the shelter half draped over my head. Yet as I continued my superhuman effort, I could feel my buttocks slide back onto the catwalk. My breathing was heavy and out of control as I pulled the shelter half from over my head and pushed it onto the catwalk ahead of me. I heard Wes shout something but I did not understand it. Instead, I looked down at the catwalk in front of me and murmured, "Thank you, God. Thank you."

I righted myself fully, and was surprised to see my suitcase riding easily ahead of me, and I recalled holding it in place with my head. As I breathed more easily I looked over at Wes. He waved an okay signal. I sat back, began to relax.

Wes called over, "We only have to hang on until Mitchell."

The wind had shifted and the soot and cinders were no longer blowing on us. Yet, as I settled back I could feel the cinder burns on my face and arms.

Finally I felt the train slowing and noticed we were entering the railroad yard in Mitchell. I expected the train to stop but it didn't, and I envisioned being pulled to the other side of town and away from Highway 90, our route west. Wes had folded his shelter half, and he called, "If you climb over here we'll jump off before we're carried too far."

I nodded, and began the dangerous move to his side of the car. I rose carefully, extended my right hand to the tank beside me, picked up my suitcase and very slowly took several steps forward, turned the corner at the end of the huge tank, stepped on the mechanism that locked the petroleum car to the one ahead of it and extended the suitcase to Wes. It was a grim operation and I could hardly get my breath. Yet I was determined to move my stuff and myself to the other side of the car so we could jump together. I repeated the operation to bring my shelter half over to Wes's side. I pushed my stuff up the catwalk in front of Wes and kneeled, positioning myself for the jump. "Let's go in just a couple of seconds," I suggested. And as I said that I shoved my luggage and jumped. Wes did the same.

We landed with a thud, not with the grace of parachute jumpers, and rolled in the cinders of the railroad bed. The sharp pain of the cinders grinding into my skin and the smell of the dust and chemical spills let me know the freight train ride was over. I collected my thoughts and realized it would be hitchhiking from here. With cinder burns smarting on my face and arms and the newly acquired abrasions from the cinders paining me, I tried to pull myself together.

"We're still in one piece!" Wes shouted. "Thank God. But look at that poor suitcase. It's all busted up. How in the hell are we going to carry our groceries?"

"No big deal," I answered. "We can get a rope or cord someplace and tie it together."

"Great. Great," Wes challenged. "Where do we get that?"

"Maybe over at that service station," I answered, pointing to a station about a hundred yards away. "And if that doesn't work out, we can put the cans in a paper box, put a handle on it and throw the suitcase away."

Wes threw his hands up in the air. "Why don't you see what you can do."

"Right," I answered, and with that I walked to the service station and described our problem to the attendant.

He paused a moment and suggested, "I've just thrown out an old extension cord. It's out back in the trash can. Help yourself."

I walked out back and retrieved the cord. It looked like it would fix the suitcase. While there I requested the use of the men's room, and used much soap, water and paper towels to clean myself and my clothes. The holes burned into my shirt and trousers stood out, but I did my best to clean them. I also put cold water on the burns on my arms and face. The results were only modest. The burns and abrasions continued to hurt. Besides, I had the appearance of someone with measles, as my skin was marked with mean looking red spots.

I felt better after I had done all of that, and I hurried back to Wes, who was sitting on the remaining intact suitcase and guarding the rest of the luggage. My good spirits were dashed when Wes charged, "Where in the hell have you been?"

"Over at the station," I answered matter-of-factly. "Got a great cord."

"Why should that take you so long?" Wes continued to press.

"Well, I stopped to clean up. Good place to do it." Before Wes could challenge me for leaving him out of the cleanup I suggested, "While I tie up the suitcase, why don't we go there and use the facility."

Wes's anger did not lift but he volunteered to hold the suitcase as I wrapped it with the extension cord. "Looks good," I commented as I tied the cord and lifted the suitcase. Wes frowned but did not answer.

There was nothing left to do so I joined Wes in his trek to the service station. I hoped that a wash-up would lift his spirits. In the meantime I shifted the conversation. "What did you think of our ride?"

"It was wild, too wild," Wes shouted. "To be truthful, I thought it was all over for us. I figured you were a goner when you were sliding off the catwalk. My God, it was a miracle that you got back on. A miracle. . . . And me too," he continued. "I figured it was all over for me a couple of times. Especially when I wrestled my suitcase and the shelter half and tried to stay on the catwalk, but my butt slid over the edge a couple of times.

There was nothing to hold on to except the catwalk itself. No rails, nothing!"

"Let's sit on the curb here for a few minutes to shake it off," I suggested.

Wes nodded and dropped to the curb. I followed and we sat in complete silence for a while, maybe fifteen minutes to a half hour, as we regained our composure. Finally Wes shifted and said, "I've got to get cleaned up. I can't take this any longer." We walked the rest of the way to the service station, taking the luggage with us.

The attendant at the station looked at us critically as Wes requested the use of the toilet. He frowned as he looked at me. "Are you bringing your whole family in here?"

I laughed gently. "No. Only one member."

His expression did not change, but he gave his reluctant, "Okay."

Soap, water and ample use of paper towels brought Wes back to almost normal. Once he was somewhat restored we left, thanking the attendant. His response was disdain. I guess he figured we were a couple of bums. We, however, could not be put down. After all, we had successfully traveled the first leg of our journey, although precariously, and were ready to move on.

Highway 90 was not far away, and after locating it we chose a spot next to a stoplight, figuring the drivers would have to look us over as we appealed for a ride, and our appearance would assure them that we wouldn't pose any danger. We put the luggage behind us, hoping to hide its condition and size from the drivers.

I encouraged Wes to move ahead of me because I figured he was a better salesman. He had a ready smile, and as he put his thumb out he made a special appeal. We were eager to move on, but the large number of cars that passed by frustrated that wish and we missed the certainty of the freight train.

Finally an old, small Ford truck approached and came to a coasting stop. An elderly man, who had several missing teeth and whose general condition matched that of the aging truck, leaned out of the cab window and in a highly pitched voice challenged, "If you boys will share the truck with the chickens, you're welcome. I am going to Plankinton, a bit up the road."

We badly needed a ride, but we were skittish about the offer. The truck looked as if it was held together by the owner's determination and help of a service station mechanic. Moreover, the suggestion that we ride with the chickens was a put-down. They stunk!

"Yep, it isn't much, but I go all the way to Plankinton—that's thirty miles. Get you boys on your way. Now where are you headed?"

"Rapid City."

"Well, I won't get you there, but I'll get you started."

I assumed that he didn't offer us seats in the cab because he was afraid of us. Yet he introduced himself, and I hoped he would change his mind. "I'm Will Jenkins. Own a farm just south of here." He nodded his head, suggesting that we make up our minds. However, he did not offer us a ride in the cab.

We hesitated as the stench of the chickens surrounded us, shrugged our shoulders, then threw the luggage into the truck bed and climbed aboard. It was less exciting than the freight train but safer, to be sure. The floor was covered with feathers, but luckily the manure was confined to the crates holding the chickens. But its stink let us know it was there.

The farmer looked back through the window, nodded his head, ground the stick shift into gear and took off. The breeze produced by the truck's forward motion blew the feathers and some of the stench out of our area, making our situation somewhat more tolerable. We huddled behind the truck cab, and as the truck picked up speed, we peered in the back window and were surprised to learn the speedometer read fifty miles per hour. The truck shook and quivered. Wes and I wondered whether it was truly safer than the freight. We sought excitement; however, this was not the kind we were looking for. At fifty miles per hour we covered the distance to Plankinton in a little over thirty minutes and were relieved when the truck pulled to the side of the road and stopped. We jumped off after having thrown our luggage off first, and shouted a "Thank you" to the farmer. He tipped his hat, waved, ground the truck's gears and was off in a cloud of blue smoke and a whirl of chicken feathers. We stood there enjoying a sense of relief and breathed deeply to get a breath of fresh air unpolluted by the smell of chickens.

"How did you like that?" I asked, mixing consternation, awe and disgust.

"Well, it was free, but pretty hard to take," Wes commented as he shook with laughter.

"In some ways it was as bad as the soot and sparks of the freight. I never feared I would fall off of the truck, but I wondered whether it would shake apart and leave us in midair!"

We looked at each other and laughed. We had feathers in our hair and smelled like a chicken coop. "That was the best chicken shit ride we'll ever have," Wes remarked. But his comment was broken, as he laughed so hard he couldn't continue.

I was in the same state, and blurted, "Chicken shit is right, and it's all over us."

"Even more powerful than the soot and sparks!" Wes added, and we continued to laugh.

People on the sidewalk near us smiled, but they had no idea about what was causing the hilarity. We finally got ourselves under control and realized we were still on Highway 90, though here in Plankinton it was also Main Street. The street was bordered by a few stores and bars with false fronts. These buildings were once fronted by hitching posts, horses, wagons and buggies. Now, however, they were fronted by cars and pickup trucks and an occasional larger truck.

Before we had reorganized ourselves, a black Chevrolet pulled alongside of us. The seal of South Dakota was emblazoned on the front doors. Gold letters spelled SOUTH DAKOTA STATE REFORMATORY.

Our concern about the police and highway patrol was heightened by the reformatory sign and the clean-cut appearance of the driver. Though he had an official air, he did not wear a uniform. In contrast, he wore freshly pressed khaki trousers and a sport shirt. His neatness made us painfully aware of our clothes, scrubbed in places and holes from the soot in others, and saturated with the stink of chicken manure. The driver did not comment or ask about our clothes or the smell, though he scrutinized us closely. Instead, he casually asked, "Where are you boys headed?"

We replied immediately, "To the Black Hills. To Rapid City."

"You're on the right highway. No doubt about that. But you must be careful of the highway patrol. They are picking up hitchhikers, detaining them for questioning. This all started after a hitchhiker kidnaped and murdered an elderly couple about a month ago. They got him all right, but now everybody is scared, and the patrol is cracking down. There's even talk about passing a law against hitchhiking. Right now they are picking up hitchhikers and charging them with loitering."

"That's got nothing to do with us," I volunteered. "We just want to see the Hills and Mt. Rushmore. Nothing more."

"Doesn't make any difference. People are scared and the patrol is trying to do its job."

We nodded and said no more, and the driver concluded, "So you boys have to be careful."

We stood at the side of his car, hoping he would ask us to join him. After looking us over again, he did not invite us in, but introduced himself. "I am Dermit Jackson. I work at the reform school as a counselor." There was a pause and he finally suggested, "One of you sit in the front with me. The other in back." He added, "Looks like you emptied your closets to make up all that luggage. Better put that in back." He raised his eyebrows when he saw the broken suitcase wrapped in an extension cord, but did not say anything.

We smiled and thought, if he knew what the suitcases held he would have said, "You emptied your pantries."

Mr. Jackson continued to scrutinize us. I had hoped that was over, as his glare made me uneasy. It was a police look, and given that he worked in the reformatory, it worried me. Then he asked, "Have you boys been out in the sun, out too long?" That wiped out the police concern.

I answered, "No, but we have had some other heat."

"How's that?" Mr Jackson asked.

Both Wes and I explained the details of our train ride. He shook his head in amazement. "My God, you're lucky to be here—lucky you're not mashed up along the railroad tracks!"

We nodded our heads in agreement as the full impact of the near catastrophe of the train ride hit us. We sat quietly as Mr. Jackson continued to shake his head. After a few moments he offered, "I went swimming over the weekend and have some sunburn lotion which should do you some good." He reached into the glove compartment of his car, pulled out a tube of lotion and handed it to me. "Put this on, all over your face. You've got a couple of bad spots. Then give it to your friend. Keep it and use it every day until your burns clear up."

To get a ride was good; however, to get such caring treatment was beyond all of our expectations and we thanked Mr. Jackson with great appreciation. He simply nodded and kept driving. We sat mostly silent while he talked.

Mr. Jackson told us about the reformatory, about some of the boys and the future plans for the place. He spoke at some length of a rehabilitation approach being used. It considered the boys' delinquency as stemming from conflicted and broken family relationships, from frustration, anger and hopelessness. The program sought to mend the boys' rebellion and deviousness through counseling, remedial education, vocational training and recreation. Mr. Jackson's enthusiasm gave the program wings. It sounded too good to be true, but we were too polite to challenge him. We wondered what the rank and file of boys thought about it.

"Now, tell me about yourselves, things other than your wanting to go to the Black Hills. Where do you go to school?"

I answered, "Sioux Center. You know, that's just above Yankton about thirty miles. We're both going to be juniors."

"I know just where it is," Mr. Jackson replied, and asked, "How well do you do in your courses?"

I hesitated a moment, wishing I could give a better report, but I gave a truthful answer. "Okay. Should be better. I only do B work. Wes does better."

Wes smiled but didn't say anything, but when Mr. Jackson asked, "What courses do you like best?" he answered, "Science courses, especially physics and chemistry, but I like all my courses, even history and English."

Mr. Jackson looked at me and I answered, "I like social studies the best. I really do." But I felt my answer was not as good as Wes's.

Mr. Jackson nodded and I could feel his sincere interest in our activities. In many ways he was like Mr. Hanson back in our civics class, always interested in what we were about. He continued, "Do you go out for any sports?"

That really tapped our interest and I said, "We've gone out for both football and basketball for a couple of years, but neither of us has made the team. Football is coming up soon and we both think we have a good chance of making the team this year."

"Sounds good," Mr. Jackson affirmed. "I admire you for staying in there. Not giving up." He paused several moments. He looked like he was thinking and then asked, "Have you fellows thought about a career? That is, what you'd like to do for an occupation?"

We figured he was used to asking the boys at the reformatory these questions. Yet we felt that he meant more than that, that he really was interested in us, and though he was asking us a lot of questions, he asked them so easily, so naturally that it was like an ordinary conversation.

Wes picked up. "I'd like to get into science, big science, at a big university where they do important research. That's what I'd really like."

"That means you've really got to bear down on your courses," Mr. Jackson commented.

Wes nodded his head and Mr. Jackson felt the depth of his commitment.

"And you?" he turned to me.

In my heart I felt I probably would become a social studies teacher in high school and coach along with that. But Wes's aims were so good I felt I had to say something better than teaching and coaching, so I said, "I've been thinking about geology. I think I'd really like that." To be truthful I did like the idea of geology, but I was afraid of the university course work necessary to become one.

Mr. Jackson nodded his head in approval and added, "I can see I've picked up a couple of serious fellows. Hard working too."

Wes and I smiled, but said nothing more.

As our conversation slowed Mr. Jackson changed his tone slightly. "I should have told you I am on my way to Kimball to pick up a runaway. The boy ran away yesterday. He only got about thirty miles before the police picked him up."

"Where is he now?" I asked.

"In jail. Not the best place for him. Rightly he should be in a juvenile detention center. But that's a nicety beyond a rural area with limited money. Further, there isn't enough traffic in juvenile delinquents in Kimball to warrant one, so he is in jail. Not the place for him, but at least he won't be running away."

"Why did he run away from the reformatory?" I followed up.

"He's new in the reformatory and too young to be there. I figure he got homesick and decided to take off, hoping to make it to Chamberlain, his home town." Mr. Jackson rubbed his chin. "I think the judge made a mistake in sending him to us. He's too young, too impressionable. Even though his dad is out of the picture and his mother doesn't want him, I think something should have been worked out for him in Chamberlain."

"What's going to happen to him when you get him back? What's the punishment?" Wes asked.

"Probably no punishment. I'll talk with him to learn what he was thinking. Then I'll talk with the staff committee—each boy has one—to see how they want to handle it. I can't predict, but I figure the committee will say, 'Put him back into the orientation dorm. Start him over.' "

"What's the orientation dorm?" Wes pursued.

"It's a unit that has a program for new boys, to help them get started, and it gives us a chance to size them up."

"How do you mean, size them up?" Wes asked.

"The dorm supervisors make observations of their behavior, how they usually do, and especially what they do under stress. The psychologist gives tests and the social worker talks with them, especially about their family life. Once in a while we get a case that needs a psychiatrist, and we call one in. But we missed on this one."

"What's the boy's name?" I asked.

"Melvin."

The miles sped by and we arrived in Kimball before we expected it. "Here we are," Mr. Jackson announced. "It didn't take long."

As we got out of the car and pulled our luggage behind us, Mr. Jackson warned in a friendly tone, "Take care of yourselves." He added, with a smile, "And your luggage too."

With that he drove off. We were sorry to see him go, yet we were inspired by his optimism and good spirits. Also, we sensed Mr. Jackson's interest in our well being.

We cast our eyes about Kimball and concluded it was a small western town like Plankinton, serving as a trade center for the surrounding country. It was surviving, but we saw so little activity we wondered how. We stood at the edge of the road and carefully thumbed each car that passed by, always being sure to offer a friendly smile. However, the cars were few and any interest the drivers might have had in us did not extend to stopping.

The ride with Mr. Jackson, though enjoyable, had been sobering, especially as we thought about Melvin. We did not know him excepting through Mr. Jackson, and then only in a small way. Wes, in deep thought, conjectured, "It must be a tough, tough situation, trying to get along when nobody wants you. The reformatory is trying to do something for him, or with him, but it doesn't really want him, you know, like a parent."

I nodded my head, but couldn't think of anything to add to what Wes had said. I worried about Melvin and wondered, "What must jail be like for him?"

"Bad," Wes answered quickly.

"I mean, how he took it."

"Bad," Wes repeated.

I rubbed my head and concluded, "And I say bad for his prospects at the reformatory."

Wes agreed but offered a ray of hope. "Maybe Mr. Jackson can make the difference."

We stood in silence, more concerned about Melvin than our hitchhiking. Finally, at about ten-thirty, a rough looking man stopped his equally rough looking car. His voice was gruff. "Where you headed?"

"The Hills and Rapid City."

"That's a long way. You aren't going to make it today. No way."

We had wondered about that ourselves, yet we were optimistic. But the gruff, overly certain voice discouraged us. When he saw gloom on our faces he spoke quickly. "Tell you what I'll do. I'll take you there. Going there myself, but it will cost you, four dollars apiece."

I wondered for a minute. It seemed like a good deal. Yet I knew our budgets couldn't take that spending. I looked at Wes and believed his evaluation was the same as mine, and he shook his head.

"Sorry," I said. "We're going to hitch it."

"It's just not a good idea. You'll not make it today. Besides, the highway patrol is picking up hitchhikers and giving them jail time. Better think it over."

The guy was getting obnoxious and we both shook our heads and walked to the side of the road.

Angered, he shouted, "You're making a mistake," and drove off.

"That guy had a lot of guts," I charged.

Wes nodded. "I had it with him."

Our agitation was smoothed a short time later when a highly polished, late model Buick stopped. I noticed its lacquered, shiny spokes. Its splendor included a good measure of chrome that framed the headlights, radiator and bumper up front, and the lights and bumper in back. An elderly couple were seated up front and the man smiled. I sensed a note of generosity.

We were overly ready to get in, and made several steps. However, the driver raised his hands gently. "Now, just a minute, boys. Not so fast." His gesture was the beginning of an inquiry that lasted for about ten minutes, but which seemed much longer. His questions were no-nonsense, threatening and personal, as if we had done something wrong. We were tolerant, matter-of-fact and dutiful, an attitude showing respect to elders. We felt put upon and felt no ride would be offered. Consequently, we were surprised when he said, "Get in and bring your stuff." We were pleased to accept, though the invitation was in the same tone that characterized his questions—matter-of-fact, tough.

He continued in a softer tone, "We are the Adams. This is my wife Alice and I'm known as Bill. I'm a school man, have been my whole life, began as a teacher and ended as superintendent of schools right here in Kimball. Did it for twenty seven years. When I was young I wanted to run something, maybe a business, or a school, something, and it turned out to be a school. I suppose because I was trained as a teacher, and I always like to work with youth. Still do, but I'm pretty much out of it now. I'm retired. Retired last spring. Yup, last year was my last one."

His was a matter-of-fact statement, one that did not invite a response. His manner was like that of the stereotype teacher— prim, precise and humorless. His thin face, beak-like nose and small sharp eyes added to his no-nonsense character. He repeated, "Yes, I am retired now. Figured I had done it long enough. Figured I'd let someone else try it."

I nodded and Wes said, "Yep."

"There were some real highlights." As Mr. Adams said this he took a firmer grip on the wheel and his eyes glazed over. "When I was first a teacher I fought for science, math and English to be required for graduation. I knew the kids who were going on to college would need it, and for those who weren't, well, it would do them some good in life. I wanted a high school certificate from Kimball High School to mean something."

Mr. Adams paused, shifted in his seat and continued, but paid no attention to us. "I got the superintendent to go along with awarding trophies to seniors for high achievement in the different subjects. We never actually gave the kids the trophies, but we had their names engraved on them and put them in a special case in the hallway. And I pushed to get the most able students scholarships at the university."

As he continued to look at us whenever his driving allowed, Mr. Adams said, "Those were all good things," and noted, "When I got to be superintendent I worked hard to get good teachers, kept the standards high and got them decent pay. So I had their loyalty and we worked to keep up a first-rate program. All in all, it was a wonderful experience, a decent way to spend my life."

Mr. Adams had made his statement and nothing more was said. We were intimidated and did not break the silence. Had I been able to speak to Wes, I would have said, "I don't think I would like being his student or being in his school. Too rigid." And I imagined Wes saying, "Hold on there. He ran a good school. It's just what you need."

We rode to Chamberlain and I wondered what would happen next on our trip. Would we continue to get rides? Would it go well? Would we get into Rapid City by the end of the day?

Mr. Adams slowed his Buick as we came into Chamberlain. It struck us as quite large. Yet we were in mid-town in about five minutes. Though Mr. Adams' sternness made me tense, I hated being dropped off again. It would make for a period of uncertainty and anxiety as we appealed for another ride. And when that ride came, we never knew who it would be with or how far it would go.

Mr. Adams broke the silence. "Boys, I'll drop you off at the next corner. There seems to be enough traffic for you to get another ride."

We agreed and when Mr. Adams said, "Goodbye," a different spirit entered his voice. It was friendly and supportive. As we left, Mrs. Adams joined him saying goodbye. It was the first time she had spoken.

I was finally able to speak my earlier thoughts. "Wes, I don't think I would have liked being a student in the Kimball school."

"Oh, I don't know. You're too hard on Mr. Adams. He's okay, but just takes himself too seriously and talks tough."

"Maybe, but I'm glad to be in Sioux Center. But I'm glad he picked us up. He helped us out."

"Enough on Mr. Adams," Wes concluded. "What did you think of the country we crossed?"

"Dry prairie, large tracts of land, a few ranches and only a few people. Not quite a desert, but almost. Reminded me of some pictures I've seen of the southwest. 'Course, no big rocks or cactus here, but in some ways it reminded me of those pictures. Not like our part of the state, which is more like the corn belt."

Wes suggested, "Let's move off the road and onto the sidewalk. No sense in getting run over. There are a lot of cars, but they look like they belong to local people out doing errands. Let's get to a toilet, then walk through town."

We passed several restaurants en route to a service station toilet, and picked up scents of the noontime meal. "I wish we could get a hamburger," Wes suggested.

"I know, I know. But our money won't allow it. We better hurry out of town and see what we can pull from the suitcase."

We did not succumb to the smell of hamburgers and french fries. Instead, we walked to the toilet and then through town. Chamberlain was larger than any town we had been in, with the exception of Mitchell. We noted its stores and shops were in better condition than those of Pukwana, Kimball or White Lake that we had passed through, and as we walked on we saw that its residential district was also more upscale.

"We should come to the Missouri River at the other side of town," Wes noted as he strained under the weight of the luggage. Especially heavy was the suitcase loaded with cans of beans and other edibles.

"I'm all for getting there," I added as I, too, felt the weight of the luggage grind into my hands and pull on my shoulder and back muscles. "I like doing this if it means getting in shape for football. But it may be more than I need."

"You wait. When the season starts and the coach gets tough, this will all seem like duck soup." Wes paused, then exclaimed, "There's the river! That's what I've been waiting for. God, it's wide, maybe half a mile."

"And it's swift. Really swift." I laughed as I said it.

"What a place to swim," Wes suggested. "But not really."

"And get drowned?" I asked.

"I know, I know. I'm for staying out of it."

26

I added, "Besides, it's a long drop down there and I'm for staying up here. Getting down there would be treacherous in itself, to say nothing about trying to swim in the river."

The Big Muddy moved swiftly about a hundred feet or more below the bluffs on which we stood. Cottonwood trees shaded the shoreline; otherwise there was nothing to interrupt the landscape of bluffs, river and trees. However, a vast expanse of near-desert land extended beyond the trees on the other side of the river.

"I'm for walking across the bridge, just for the experience. Even if we miss a ride, we can always catch a ride on the other side."

Wes agreed. We picked up our luggage and started across the bridge. It was a huge steel structure. Its massiveness helped us feel safe. Still, we kept our distance from the guardrail—indeed, a couple of yards from it. Cars sped past us. A couple of them blew their horns as we forced them into the left lane by our liberal domination of the right lane. We just didn't want to get close to the edge of the bridge.

"This beats hitchhiking," Wes called out as we got close to the other side. "Only took us about twenty minutes. That cars passed us, cars which might have picked us up on the highway, doesn't bother me."

We enjoyed the walk. I spied a picnic table in a small park at the end of the bridge and suggested, "Let's stop over there."

Immediately after we stopped Wes said, "This will be the first meal of this mighty trip. But it seems like a long time ago that we left home."

"Yeah," I called out to toast the situation. "Yeah!"

Wes removed the extension cord from the suitcase. He bit his lips. "This damn suitcase looks sad with the extension cord around it, but I guess we can live with it." He pulled a can of beans and some bread from the suitcase and opened the can. We pulled spoons from our hip pockets and passed the beans back and forth between us until the can was slick and clean. Chunks of bread were eaten between the spoonfuls of beans, and everything tasted so good. Wes concluded, "That was a banquet!"

27

I wired the suitcase back together and we hurried back to the road. It wasn't quite one o'clock. Our morale was high. We had come almost halfway to Rapid City and envisioned being there by the day's end. However, our hope for an early ride vanished. A few cars passed, but none stopped. We reasoned, "It's lunchtime and the traffic will pick up soon." Yet such did not happen. Another hour went by and we still were on the side of the road waiting and waiting. I wondered if we had missed a ride by walking across the bridge, but that had passed and could not be changed.

It was very hot, perhaps ninety-five degrees or so, and the sun beat down on us without mercy. "God, it's hot!" Wes complained. "My head hurts and my mouth is so dry it feels like cotton. I'd do anything for a drink."

I nodded but was too hot to complain.

We were aware that a work crew was up the road about a half mile.

Wes suggested, "Let's walk up there and see if we can get a drink. They surely have water with them."

I picked up my gear as Wes did his and we started down the road, keeping our thumbs up as cars passed us, but no one stopped. The pavement burned with heat and we walked on the shoulder of the road, on dirt, to reduce the heat. As we looked up the highway to judge the distance to the work crew, heat waves danced on the road like those one can see coming off a hot grill. The heat was so intense it nearly brought us to our knees, but we finally got there.

The work crew did not greet or even recognize us as we approached. Instead they continued to work as if we were just another negative part in their bad situation. Theirs was a miserable task—pouring boiling tar onto the road, spreading it and raking crushed rock over it. The intense heat of the tar and the heavy work, coupled with the heat of the day, sapped whatever good spirits they may have had. At any rate, they ignored us.

Mustering courage I asked the man closest by, "Might you have some water?"

He raised his head and looked at me with a sullen stare. Sweat poured down his face even though his head was wrapped in a bandana, tied in the style of a turban. Without any change in his expression he simply nodded his head in the direction of a barrel on the back of a truck. None of his associates bothered to raise their heads. A couple of teenage kids were the furthest from their concern. Indeed, we were an annoyance.

The water was so warm it was almost hot, but we drank with relish and only stopped to catch our breath. We nodded to each other when we had our fill, and thanked the man in charge but he said nothing. We followed the road for about fifty yards and decided it was a good spot to continue our hitchhiking. We assumed that cars would slow down for the highway repair, notice us and stop, but we were wrong. The cars slowed down for the highway repair, noticed us but did not stop to pick us up. We waited and waited for over an hour. The sun continued to beat down on us and we were about to walk back for another drink. We clearly needed relief.

"Let's go back for more water," I urged. "They are a grim, angry-looking bunch, but we need water."

"We can tough it out," Wes argued. "I don't want to challenge them in any way. We did right by drinking the water, thanking them and getting out of there. I don't want to go back."

I was blunt. "We need water. It's the only place there is any. We'll be okay if we don't offend them."

Reluctantly Wes agreed. "If you say so."

"Let's go and tread lightly. I think we'll be okay."

We picked up our luggage and struggled back to the work crew. I was about to ask for more water when the foreman glared at us. "I thought we were rid of you an hour ago. What the hell are you doing back here?"

"The heat got to us," I answered matter-of-factly, but with a tone of meekness. "We're awfully thirsty."

"What in the hell do you need water for? You're not doing any work."

"Well," I stammered, "well . . . the sun is getting to us."

The foreman wiped the sweat off his face and with disgust said, "All right. But don't be drinking it all, and I don't want to see you back here again."

Wes and I had a big drink, then thanked the foreman. He did not acknowledge it and we left.

When we reached our former spot we dropped our luggage. The dull thud it made as it hit the ground was a good measure of our beaten-down spirits, spirits that were in the dust.

"I don't know what the hell was eating on that guy. He had a whole barrel of water," Wes charged. "More than enough for the work crew."

I added, "To hell with him."

Our anger was distracting and we failed to see the car that pulled up, but a very loud, "Hey, hey, hey," got our attention. We turned and faced a large, unkempt, fierce man. He continued, "I won't try to sell you a couple seats in my car, but you're welcome to them. I figure that's what you're after. Yes, sir, they are the best seats between here and Kennebec. And let me tell you something else. If you expect to get a ride you have to get your thumbs up. Really go after it."

I read the sign on the door—WILD BILL: CHAMPION AUCTIONEER OF INSPIRED SALES—when he repeated his very loud, "Hey, hey, hey," and added, "You better get in before I change my mind."

Caught up by Wild Bill's enthusiasm, we jumped into his car, luggage and all. I had scanned the car's cardinal red paint job on our way into the car. I decided it was one Wild Bill had done himself. There were just too many places where amateur brush strokes stood out. Yet it was a masterful job of covering the fifteen or so years of the car's history.

Wild Bill repeated, "The best two seats between here and Kennebec." He pounded on the steering wheel. "I've been nursing this baby along for about sixteen years. That's right, sixteen years. Been following my mission even longer. A good mission, if I say so myself. Always do my best to get the best price for my clients. That's what auctioneering is all about. Yes, sir!"

He caught his breath but did not hesitate. "If you're settled I'll take off." He had barely managed the gear shifting when he asked, "What brings you fellows out here? You know you're in the West, don't you?"

Before we could answer he observed, "You fellows look like you're from the East. You don't wear jeans or blue work shirts, and I don't see any cowboy boots on you. And, as you ran to get into the car I didn't see any stride like fellows who ride horses. No, I didn't see any of those things."

As Wild Bill was checking the speedometer I answered his question, asked some time ago. "We're going to see Mt. Rushmore and the sights in the Hills."

"That's a mighty fine thing for you boys to be doing. I've said that same thing to myself many times. That is, I've said, 'Bill, take some time, take a vacation, get out and see what's around you.' But you know, I just don't pay any attention to myself, even when I add, 'Do it before it's too late.' No, I don't. I don't pay any attention to my own warnings. I just keep working, just keep plying my trade. If you didn't see my sign on the door," and he patted the door with his hand, "I am an auctioneer! That's right, I'm one of those fellows who works for a living. I never stop promoting my work. I advertise. I put out the word constantly through my friends, and anyone who will listen. And when I get a job I'm Johnny- on-the-spot, getting the sale organized, getting the notices out, getting the church women to get a lunch counter set up, sell coffee, that kind of thing. Yeah, I work hand-in-glove with them. They are good people. Good!"

"How does the actual auctioneering go?" I hurried to ask. "What do you say? What is your sing-song lingo?"

"Now you're getting right to it. Right to it. When I get up on the auctioneer's stand I'm raring to go, ready to do business. I feel like I'm a politician speaking to a crowd at election time. I feel like I have some convincing to do. I know that, so I get right to it. I give the crowd a little warmup, say a few good things about them, a few good things about the quality of the stuff that I will be selling, and most important, I give them a pep talk about getting with the sale, to take part, to take some valuable things away with them. In simple language, I try to get them into a buying mood."

Wes and I had settled back into our seats, resigned to Bill's performance. Yet we were careful to keep interested expressions on our faces because we saw Bill eyeing us through the rear view mirror.

His talk continued. "I'm sorry to see you boys are hell-bent on getting to the Hills, or I judge that you are. Because you might enjoy coming out to the auction with me. Yes, I think you would enjoy the whole thing—the crowd, the church ladies, the excitement, the smell of the food, the owner. Yes, you would enjoy the spirit of the whole thing."

I apologized. "Sounds good, very good, but we need to push on. So we thank you but we'll keep trying for rides."

Obviously disappointed, Wild Bill cleared his throat, blinked and sniffed. After shifting in his seat he picked up his previous bluster. "Now you boys look like you're of high school age."

We nodded and Bill picked it up in the mirror. He continued. "That's a good age, couldn't be better, the best age to be. I remember when I was your age I was one hell of a ballplayer, especially a hell of a football player. I ran the ball, made big plays. I threw passes. I could do it all. I played both ways—offense and defense. And let me tell you when I tackled the opposition runners I really hit them. I not only stopped them cold but I made them think before they came at me again."

I saw a road sign that read three miles to Kennebec. Bill must have seen it too, because he hurried his talk. "I was offered a college scholarship. In fact, several of them, and I would like to have gone, but my dad said it was time to go to work. I didn't like it but I didn't argue with him. I've often thought I should have, but I didn't. Nobody in his family had ever gone to college. It just wasn't in his bones. Yep, I went to work after graduating, in a warehouse, moving, lifting, packing stuff of all kinds. But then I got into this auctioneering. I like it. I'm proud of it, and plan to stay with it."

Wes pressed to ask our most serious question, "Just how do you do that special auctioneer's lingo, or whatever you call it?"

"Well, boys, that's a part of the auctioneer's magic. Closest I can describe it, it's a combination of a growl, a call, a slur that comes from deep in the throat, at least the first part of the call for a bid. Now every auctioneer has his own particular style. I always start with an 'aw, ow,' a sound to get attention. I move it fast, and blend into 'What am I offered?' I repeat that, to put a little rhythm into it. Then I add 'Who'll start it off at $20,' or whatever I think is reasonable. Then I break into the next higher price, and so on. But don't misunderstand me. The special bark of the auctioneer is just one part of the deal. To tell you the truth, I throw my whole self into it—my hands, eyes, my whole body. Then, of course, I growl out my auctioneer's lingo. Let's say I'm trying to get a couple bidders to move above a hundred dollars but the bidding has stalled. If I can't get anything above a hundred and the item is clearly worth more, I may stop, pause, let quiet settle over the crowd. Then I'll go into a description about the fine quality of the thing being auctioned. Let's say it's a quality chandelier. I'll tell them it's worth at least three times what is being offered. I may even use a little down-at-the-nose attitude to shame them for their conservative offers. I'm polite, of course. Can't do it any different. Then I break into my auctioneer lingo, pushing the price up to one hundred and fifty. You got to use the auctioneer's lingo, even though it's a little mumbo-jumbo. It gives the bidding some style."

Wes enthused, "Great."

I didn't know whether he meant it but Wild Bill did and he broke into an enthused response. "You've got it! You've got it!"

I timed my question, interjecting it into Wild Bill's torrent of words. "Where did you learn how to auctioneer? I mean, put that warble into your voice?"

Wild Bill was pleased with the question. "Son, I went off to an auctioneering college for two weeks in Sioux City, Iowa. No, it's not a part of Morningside College. You know, that's down there too, don't you?" He asked the question with pride, and I sensed he was showing off his academic associations. "No, it's a college all by itself. It took some convincing of myself to go there. I mean, I had to push myself to do it. Well, I came up with the money, sent in my application and they said 'Come ahead.' I went. There were about two dozen of us in the class. I got along fine because I like to talk, but I just couldn't get into the swing of that auctioneer's bark. I got so discouraged I went home after the first week, figuring on quitting. I wasn't going back no how."

There was a break in his talk so I broke in. "So what did you do?"

"My wife and kids got on me. They told me I could do it, if I just made up my mind to it."

He paused and I asked, "So what did you do?"

"I went back. Wife and family were counting on me, and by God I did it! When the class graduated after one more week, I was with them, got a certificate, joined in a big party and was an auctioneer!"

Wild Bill smiled and in triumph added, "Yes, siree! Had our pictures taken, shook hands all the way around and I went home like a king."

We were approaching Kennebec. I was tempted to ask if he had any tips about playing linebacker, but my inclination was stopped cold by Wild Bill's final blast. "Well, you boys will be sorry for skipping my sale, but that's reality." His voice trailed off as he pulled the car to the side of the road. Wes and I scrambled out. Wild Bill shouted, "I'll miss you," as he drove away.

"There's going to be one hell of a sale here in Kennebec today!" Wes exclaimed. "Especially if Wild Bill has any influence."

"What a blast of words, what a blast of emotions, what a blast of ideas!" I shouted.

"What I liked best about the whole thing was his demonstration of an auctioneer's growl and lingo, or whatever you call it. He ran it up and down the scale, almost like a musician, and put in his special drawl into it."

I concluded, "We may have made a mistake in skipping the sale. It would be great to see him in action. But all in all we're best off staying with the hitching."

Wes nodded and we positioned ourselves on the side of the road. We were prepped by Wild Bill to take action on something, anything, but there wasn't anything we could do but stand on the road and wait for a ride, and throw rocks at a telephone pole about twenty yards away.

Our frustration and the forty minutes before another car approached gave us plenty of opportunity to scar the telephone pole next to the road. The car turned out to be an old Chrysler with a rusty body. We were eager for a ride, so the car's poor appearance did not dampen our thumbing, and we were encouraged by the driver positioning himself close to the side window and smiling. However, as the car passed us, the smile turned to a smirk and he imitated our thumbing wildly.

"You S.O.B.," Wes shouted and repeated shouting, "S.O.B.! S.O.B.!"

Irritated, I joined in the shouting. The driver heard our jeering, turned his car around and came back at us, picking up speed en route. I couldn't believe what was happening as the car came directly at us. Through some good fortune we had enough time to jump into the safety of the ditch before the car roared by. Not satisfied with his one shot at us he wheeled his car around and came back. We stayed safely crouched in the ditch as he swerved his car as close to us as he could. He leaned on the horn and it blared a threatening blast when he whizzed by.

As the car sped down the road Wes and I crawled out of the ditch. "That S.O.B.," Wes uttered. "It's a good thing our luggage was in the ditch and he didn't hit it." That summed up the situation.

Fortunately, soon after, an official-looking car with BUREAU OF INDIAN AFFAIRS painted on its front door pulled up. Without preliminaries the driver asked, "Where are you headed?"

We gave our old answer, "The Black Hills. Rapid City."

"I can take you to Murdo. That's about fifty miles from here. I cut off there to go south to Mission. I work for the Bureau down there." He paused just a minute, and added, "I'm Bill Reston. Get in and we'll get under way. It's too hot to stay in this place."

Wes and I didn't hesitate a second as we threw our luggage into the back seat. All the pain of our wait was forgotten. We were off and our spirits soared.

Wes expressed our common sentiment. "We are really glad to see you. I figured we would never get a ride and we would be better off to go back home, back to Sioux Center."

I nodded and Mr. Reston only smiled. His face was square-like, rugged in the shape of a serious westerner. "So you were about ready to hang it up?"

We nodded our heads.

"Fifty miles up the road should help you. It's only four-thirty. With luck you might make it to Rapid tonight. But you'll need some luck."

We were weary of being interviewed so I turned the tables on Mr. Reston and asked, "Just what do you do on the reservation?"

"Not a whole lot," Mr. Reston chuckled. "I have an administrative job. But I do more than push papers. In fact, I do as little of that as I can. I don't know how familiar you are with the plight of the Indians, but it's bad. They don't have much, if any, money, so their housing is bad, their clothes are poor—not quite rags but in some cases next to it—and whether they have food is always a touch-and-go matter."

Mr. Reston grimaced and went on. "They don't have any useful skills, that is, the kind that will draw industry to the reservation. It's grim. Alcoholism is common, and child neglect and abuse are more than occasional. As you may know, the Indians down at Mission are Sioux. I guess you can say the problems they face are about the same that any people without money have, excepting there are two major differences."

He grimaced again. "One is cultural—that is, the Sioux, like other Indians, come from a very unique background whose customs, traditions and beliefs are different and often in conflict with the modern world. Another is, the land on which they live is not productive. It's not fertile and the rainfall is inadequate. And, as I said earlier, there is no industry on the reservation."

Mr. Reston's spirits dropped as he told us that about the Sioux. "It's grim," he repeated. "There's an attitude problem. The Sioux men are raised in the tradition of hunters and warriors, and those interests do not mix with farming, ranching or business."

Mr. Reston's voice raised as he talked on. He seemed to be talking to someone other than Wes and me, maybe to an audience at a news conference, or even a group of legislators. It was his tone and language that made him appear that way.

He continued. "They don't want to change. They don't try to adapt. In plain language, they resist."

Mr. Reston, who had hunched over the steering wheel, relaxed and sat back. After rubbing his forehead he shifted to a more optimistic tone. "The culture has changed some, and the people with it. Yes, some change and adaptation have taken place. The major problem is the lack of opportunity. If they had that, many of the other problems would disappear."

He turned to us momentarily. "So, boys, keep these things in mind when you get back to Sioux Center. Tell your folks, tell your teachers and your friends."

We had listened with concern, now nodded our heads to his appeal, but still wanted Mr. Reston to tell us what he actually did. Our expressions must have given us away as Mr. Reston said, "So you want to know what I do?"

We smiled but did not answer.

"Well, I keep the agency office running, just to keep life going there—be sure the people are not starving, be sure the people have fuel and are not freezing, be sure kids are going to school and are not being kicked around by their parents."

He stopped, thought a minute, frowned and we thought he recalled a bad case, but he did not bring it out, yet in a moment he talked further. "I also work with the tribal police. We have to keep law and order; otherwise the whole system will break down. I encourage the chief and council that oversees his work to be consistent, to enforce the law, not be punitive—overall, take a peace-keeping approach." Mr. Reston paused and asked, "Do you want to hear more?"

We nodded.

"We're trying to bring some business in for employment, and we're trying to bring some training to develop the right kinds of skills."

"Has anything good happened?" I asked. "It sounds good."

"We've gotten an electronics assembly plant to locate here and we're starting a training program next month to train the workers. We are also going to start remodeling an old building that we already have to accommodate the plant." Mr. Reston's tone was modest and he observed, "We'll have to work hard and do our best to make it succeed. It's got to come out right."

We were interested in his earlier comment about culture. We had heard of the idea in our civics class but we knew next to nothing about it. So we asked, "What is this thing you call culture, and what kind of things does that include?"

"That's a big order, and an important one. Let me give you an example that will grab you. Are you ready?"

We nodded and Mr. Reston began. "The victory by the Indians at Little Big Horn didn't last long. The U.S. government sent a large cavalry reinforcement into what had been Indian territory. It became futile for them to resist. In 1881 Sitting Bull and his band of weary and hungry followers were forced to surrender to the U.S. Army. The glory that had briefly been the Sioux's was over. The people were made wards of the government and forced onto reservations, God-forsaken places of barren land on which no crops would grow.

"To make matters worse, the government cut back the amount of money set aside for reservations. Money to provide food and other items of care evaporated. Besides, the government pressured the Indians to sell off portions of any good land to white settlers. Starvation was common."

Mr. Reston asked, "You still with me? Not bored?"

We nodded our heads to say we were still with him and shook them to indicate we were not bored. "Just like civics class," Wes noted.

Mr. Reston talked on. "During this very hard time the Sioux were taken in by news that an Indian medicine man in Nevada had a vision in which the white settlers disappeared and the Indians who had been killed returned from the dead. The people's plight was so bad, and their beliefs in visions so strong, they accepted this overly simple vision. Believers, and there were quite a few, took part in communal dancing and chanting, which went on for days. All to bring that vision to reality. This was a part of their culture, way of believing and acting."

He continued. "Let me tell you more. The Bureau and whites were scared to death by this ceremony, called the 'Ghost Dance.' They feared the Indians would rise up and fight. So in 1890 troops were sent to Pine Ridge Reservation to stop all Ghost Dancing. Military intervention was part of the white culture of handling problems. At any rate, the whites were in a panic and the government too. However, the dancing continued. The dancers would whirl around and around, dressed up in Ghost Dance shirts, until they fell down in a trance. When they awoke they told of having seen the buffalo coming back, dead Indians coming back to life and having seen the white man's settlements roll up like a carpet, and an unspoiled prairie return—all part of the Indians' culture, their customary way of believing, doing and interpreting things."

We nodded.

He continued to explain. "Everybody was really whipped up, and it got worse when Sitting Bull, who supported the Ghost Dance movement and keeping the old Indian way of life, was killed. It began with an effort to arrest him and take him into custody because he was seen as a trouble maker. The police drove him out of his cabin, only partly dressed. At first he offered no resistance, but then a women challenged his passivity and advocated resisting. Sitting Bull accepted the challenge and shook off the police. The police followed with gunfire and he was killed. The story goes that Sitting Bull's horse appeared on the scene and began to dance. Earlier, Sitting Bull had been a member of Buffalo Bill Cody's Wild West Show, and Cody had given him a circus horse that could dance. As soon as the horse heard the gunfire it thought that a show was about to begin and went into its circus routine. So there wasn't anything mystical about it, but people believed there was."

Mr. Reston's voice changed from a story teller and instructor to his plain self. "Boys, I cut off for the Rosebud Reservation at the town ahead and that's Murdo. It's not the end of the story, but we've run out of time." He slowed and then stopped. We jumped out, took our luggage with us and waved goodbye. Mr. Reston returned our goodbye and we were back on our own.

"What a great guy," Wes exclaimed.

"I felt like I was in our civics class, or maybe social studies," I added with real enthusiasm.

We looked about us and noted that Murdo was small. That was not new to us, but it did mean few local people might drive to the next town or further on. Wes spotted a drinking fountain. "Boy, I need that. I thought I was going to pass out back there. You know, where the road crew was." With that we moved as fast as our luggage would allow to the water fountain and drank our fill. It was located on a street corner on what looked like Main Street.

"I'm ready for another ride. It's about five o'clock and we don't have any time to waste," I said.

Murdo was the most western town we had seen. That is, it most closely matched what we had seen in the movies, with false store fronts, weather beaten siding, rough shingles and occasional boardwalks. We were sorry we didn't have time to look around and absorb some of its character, but we were in a hurry, and as we looked down the road we saw the surrounding land was vast, dry, dusty prairie, badly in need of rain.

We figured that with a stroke of good luck we could still make it to Rapid City. A small Ford pickup truck stopped about fifteen minutes later. Signs on its doors, COLLINS APPLIANCE, indicated its driver was an appliance repairman and unlikely to be driving to Rapid City. A young man called out in a nasal tone, "Howdy! I'm Ken Collins." His greeting suggested he was a down-home type of fellow. He continued in a kidding voice, "What the hell are you fellows doing out here in this God-awful, windblown, dry-as-dust place? And with all that luggage?"

We went through our Rapid City, Black Hills routine and he answered, "You might just be able to make it, if you get a good ride or two. I'm not able to do that for you. But I'll take you into the heart of the Badlands. You should be able to get a ride out of there. I turn off there to make a service call about ten miles south of there. A customer's washing machine has gone bad. All in all

I can carry you about sixty miles. So if it's sightseeing you want, I can help you on that. You'll soon see."

We jumped into the cab, and after we had explained ourselves a bit further, he started down the road. Ken Collins' relaxed face tensed as he struggled with the exceptionally loose steering gear and an unruly motor which required his close management. Ken's rangy body and long arms helped him wrestle his reluctant creature. "If you boys will just put up with Old Betsy, we'll make it. Don't worry. She's never failed me. Though I have had my moments."

We nodded our heads in acknowledgment. The motor was too noisy for conversation. Further, we were happy to remain silent. We had told our story so often we were tired of it. Yet, the people were reasonable in asking. They were curious about whom they had picked up.

About an hour later we began to see peculiar formations appear on the harsh landscape. Some appeared to be huge mounds; others were more sharply shaped. All had different strata of colors. Collins shouted above the roar of the motor, removing his hands from the steering wheel and gesturing wildly, "Here they are! They are made of limestone and some special clay. Minerals give them different colors—red, purple, pink, gray, brown and tan. Nothing consistent. They are mixed up from peak to peak."

We nodded to show our enthusiasm and Collins added, after putting his hands back on the steering wheel, "Erosion caused by the wind and occasional rains cut those ravines in there that you see."

Jagged spires and pinnacles, massive buttes, mixed sharp ridges, steep-walled canyons, gullies, pyramids and knobs all crowded themselves into our view.

"Hundreds of acres of that beauty! One hundred and sixty square miles, to be exact," Ken shouted. "That's real, real beauty. You can't hear it in here because of the engine noise but the wind cries out there, sobbing and whining like a forlorn child."

41

Wes and I looked and looked in wonder. Not even the colored pictures we had seen captured the exceptionally weird formations and dramatic colors.

"There's a lot of history there," Collins continued to shout. Now his voice carried more the tone of a lecturer and less that of a carnival barker. "This area was once covered by the ocean. If not the ocean then at least a large, large body of water. Scientists have dug in there and found evidence of that. You know, evidence of sea life, and they've found dinosaur bones in there too. I don't know how that all fits together. Maybe the evidence comes from two different time periods. You know, millions of years ago."

Wes and I cheered in our excitement. After a hard day we finally felt the hoped-for excitement. We had to contain our excitement because the truck made it too noisy to talk. But we smiled, gestured and made several loud comments to show our feelings.

We rode along easily, appreciating the sights for several miles, but were jolted by Ken Collins announcing, "I turn off ahead a mile down the road. It's not the exact bottom of the Badlands but it's close to it. There's a crossroads there and you should be able to get a ride." We hoped Ken's optimism would turn out to be true and prepared to get out of the truck.

He shook our hands as he came to a stop and we pulled our belongings out with us. As Collins turned south we began to take in our location. Not only did the Badlands tower above us, but the heat was stifling. The crossroad was nothing more than a country gravel road joining Highway 90. The prospect of cars coming from there was small. The straightaway of Highway 90 was likely to carry cars at high speed and reluctant to stop. It was not only the low point of the Badlands but the low point of our feelings.

Any shred of exhilaration at being in the Badlands melted under the extreme heat. Our thirst became intense, tightened our throats and turned the insides of our mouths to cotton. We lamented for not bringing canteens, but at the time of our planning we had felt they would be too heavy. Besides, we reasoned that we could always find a place to get a drink.

Cars passed us, many of them, but none stopped. Our hopes of reaching Rapid City fell steadily as the afternoon passed. Indeed, we wondered whether we would get out of there before nightfall. We considered spending the night there if we couldn't get a ride, though it was an unlikely campground without water.

In our distress we attacked Collins. Wes led off. "That guy really left us in the lurch. No crossroad to speak of. The cars on 90 are going too fast to stop."

I added, "They don't even slow down to look us over!"

"He sure built up our hopes," Wes concluded, and we left it at that.

It was about eight o'clock. We had spent about two hours in this hot, desolate spot. Our spirits were on rock bottom. In our desperation we began to hitchhike both ways, figuring if we could not advance we would retreat. We needed water and we needed to get out of there before nightfall.

The first car that stopped was going to Kadoka, about ten or fifteen miles east. That meant retreat.

"Get in," a very alert young man encouraged. "I'll take you to the finest little town in the west, Kadoka. I'm going to be teaching social studies there this year. It's my first year out of Spearfish Teachers College. My name is Dan Larson."

Before we could acknowledge that, he talked on. "I just graduated last week, at the end of summer school. I have my degree and I'm out to make my mark."

That explained his enthusiasm, as well as his attractive casual clothes and even his highly polished glasses. That he was verbal and enthusiastic was clear. In addition, he had vivid blue eyes and medium brown hair. At about age twenty-two, he looked seventeen or eighteen, and his smile hinted of a boy who had grown up in a supporting, loving environment.

"That's great," Wes replied, and I agreed. We struggled to muster enthusiasm for Spearfish, social studies and teaching because we were preoccupied with thirst and thoughts of water. But we tried.

Dan Larson did not catch our condition and continued. "Since this is my first job I'm getting there early, getting settled so I can take off with my work the first day of classes." He paused, glanced at us as long as he could, considering his driving responsibilities. "By the way, I didn't get your names."

"Wes and Carl," I answered. "We're from Sioux Center, south of Mitchell, and we are on our way to see the Black Hills."

Dan glanced at us, sweeping his eyes over us for longer than good driving habits would allow. We thought he was being critical of our clothes, or perhaps our dehydration from being out in the sun so long. But he surprised us. "You must be at the point of choosing a college, and thinking about such."

"We are only going to be juniors come September," I said, hoping that would slow his enthusiasm. "College is not what we've been attending to."

However, such was not the case as Dan came back, "That's just the right age to begin looking around, see where you might like to go, and go after information. Maybe even college deals, depending on what you have to offer." He enthused further, "And Spearfish is a place you really must put on your list. It really is! It's a great place, offers a full range of courses, has a democratic campus atmosphere, lots of activities, and if you're athletes, it would have a special place for you."

Though we had yet to make our high school team, Dan had touched a strong point in our thoughts of the future. I followed up, "What makes it a special place for athletes?"

"They'll give you room, board and a job so you can buy your books, pay your tuition, lab fees and have a little spending money. That is, if you're really good. What's more, if you are really good, you know, in basketball or football, they might scout out a summer job for you. You'd have to work, but it would be a job."

"So they give financial help? That's for sure?" I asked. It sounded too good to be true to my inexperienced ears.

"Sure. Especially if you're good. While you're out here you ought to look up Bill Browning. He's the coach, runs the whole setup. 'Course, you have to have your high school coach's recommendation and you've got to have something to back up your claims, like being all-conference, or better yet, all-state running back, center, or whatever position you play. But don't worry. Browning will put you through that."

We liked what we heard but realized the entire unreality of the discussion, and diverted Dan to talk about the campus and Spearfish. We had yet to make our high school team, and the notion of being all-state was over our heads. As Dan drove along at a moderate speed, we recalled our earlier route, but in reverse order, and were depressed by our loss of ground.

We reached Kadoka about eight-thirty, but the sun was still out and we figured that it would remain light until about nine o'clock. We were encouraged by that.

"So you figure you'll try again today, hitchhike all the way to Rapid City?" Dan asked.

"We'd like to. We'll have to see. We're kind of beat," I replied. "We've been at it since five o'clock this morning. Then too, the heat has gotten to us."

We thanked Dan and he bid us farewell with a final encouragement. "Don't forget Spearfish Teachers."

We laughed in good spirits and Dan drove away.

"Geez, I really hated to make that retreat," Wes lamented.

"You and me both," I agreed. "It was a hell of a thing to do. Be we couldn't have survived out there much longer, and we couldn't camp out without water."

We walked a short distance to a park and drank and drank water from a public fountain. We remained there for about a half hour, going back to the fountain several times. Neither of us suggested going back on the road. We were discouraged and weary.

We applied more of Mr. Reston's lotion to our burns. The sun had dried out the earlier application and the burns were stinging. The lotion felt good and we said kind things about Mr. Reston.

Kadoka was very small. The smallness was reassuring and relaxed us. We could see the depot from where we sat. Recalling the certainty of freight train riding, we walked to the depot to make inquiries. We pushed aside its dangers. The walk was short; however, we slowed as we drew closer. We feared asking the agent about freight schedules. Finally, however, we took a direct approach and walked directly to the depot and through its door. Simple wooden benches lined the walls. Interspersed among them were several stained brass spittoons. A few dated magazines rested on one of the benches. The room was dimly lit and we squinted to see three lonely pictures hung on the walls, all showing mighty engines steaming along never-ending tracks pulling a long line of cars. The one hanging over the agent's ticket window was larger and more grand than the other two, and depicted a powerful smoking engine pulling brightly colored passenger cars over a large, trestle-supported bridge spanning a raging river far below. It was a sight to excite the viewer, especially one from the dry plains of South Dakota. It fired our imaginations in spite of the practical problem of being unable to pay for such a ride.

The agent saw our hesitation and asked, "What can I do for you boys?"

He was friendly and receptive so I asked directly, "When's the next freight to Rapid City?"

"About midnight," he replied easily. "But if you want to go to Rapid City, and be sure to get there, why not take the passenger out of here at ten o'clock? It will be clean, dry and you won't have to worry about hobos." He pressed on, but was less than a super salesman. "The tickets are only three dollars apiece. Can't beat that." He ended with, "It will get you there before midnight."

Wes and I looked at each other. We agreed with the agent's sales talk and were tempted to say, "Sure, we'll go for it." But three dollars apiece meant a good fraction of our purse. So we reluctantly shook our heads.

The agent was disappointed and so were we. Our journey had just begun and we realized there would be many demands on our funds. The agent continued, "Remember, you won't have any trouble with the passenger. In fact, it caters to your comfort. With a freight you never know what to expect. It's dangerous."

We knew he was speaking the truth and it rang clear with our experience, especially riding the catwalk on the freight to Mitchell and the problem with the sparks and burning soot. But our limited budget and long journey ahead caused us to shake our heads and lower them to avoid eye contact with him.

"Okay." The agent ended his effort, smiled a friendly smile and went to the other side of his office to attend the telegraph receiver that had a message coming in.

We walked outdoors. "Geez," I exclaimed, "I wish we could take that passenger. We'd get in there tonight, and we wouldn't have any worries."

Wes agreed and empathized, "I know, I know. But if we spend at that rate, we'll never make it all the way around the whole trip."

I nodded my head glumly and said, "Let's go back to the park and have something to eat. What would you say to beans, peaches and bread?"

"Sounds good to me."

As we arrived at the park Wes complained, "This damned cord is a hell of a nuisance. We have to untangle it every time we want something to eat."

"It's a small price to pay. It really is." I encouraged, "We're lucky the whole thing, including the food, wasn't crushed."

Wes shrugged and we dropped the matter.

We ate leisurely, drank lots of water, sat around for awhile and then walked back to the depot to wait for the midnight freight. As we sat on the bench outside the depot for a while I remarked, "You know, we haven't smoked for over a week, ever since we began doing the odd jobs to raise cash for this trip." As I considered the matter, I had the greatest urge for a smoke. "I really would like to light one up, and do it now!"

"It would be great," Wes agreed. "It's been a hard day, and not going to get any easier. So a smoke would really help us along. I didn't pack any cigarettes. Figured we didn't need them. Besides, we've got to quit before football season starts."

I picked up. "They say Williams is a tough coach. Doesn't put up with any nonsense, strict as hell. I heard from Chris Kovaleski. He's a senior and gets the word on everything. So Williams will be tough on training and conditioning."

"He was one hell of a player at the university two or three years ago and did a big job at Lesterville before getting the job at Sioux Center. I think he led Lesterville to a conference championship."

"I don't really like the guard position, but that's what I'm going for. That spot is unfilled due to graduation and I figure I'll have a good chance there. I'd rather be in the backfield and run the ball, but I know I don't have a chance there with Esworthy and Hughes coming back. So that's what I'm going to do. Go for guard."

Wes challenged the point of view. "I don't care if Esworthy and Hughes are coming back. I'm going for running back or whatever you call it. I figure I'm as fast as they are and I'm tougher, and I'm still growing. I'll give it all I've got. Besides, Williams is new and won't know much more about Esworthy and Hughes than he does about me. I'm sure he'll say all the positions are open to competition and let all of us fight for them, and I'm ready for that. I'll give them all the fight they are looking for. Yeah, I plan to let them have it."

I nodded, liked his spirit but figured the backfield was too crowded and I could punch all of the people around that I wanted to in the guard position. Besides, I had read about the great guard at the university, Ted Atkins from Tyndall, just twenty miles down the road from Sioux Center. My brother played against him. He was fast, played offense and defense, made blocks and played sixty minutes. I wanted to be like Ted Atkins—a rough, tough, volatile player. I looked forward to challenging whoever might try out for the position. I envisioned pulling a bright orange jersey over my shoulder pads, pads which exaggerated my size, and pulling on a helmet to emphasize my fierceness. Moreover, I looked forward to the brightly colored orange and black striped sox and heavily cleated shoes. Covered with that armor I would humble anyone who sought my position. Such was not only my outward attitude but my inside one too.

Wes brought me back to reality. "Let's go inside. It's getting cold out here, and darkness has crept over us without our even noticing."

The agent smiled as we entered, "Have you boys decided to take the passenger? Sure make it easier and take the worry out of traveling."

We smiled but did not answer.

"It's nice and warm in here," Wes observed. To me his statement suggested it would be a cold night on the freight. We pulled our jackets out of the suitcases and couldn't believe the radical change in the temperature since the horrible afternoon heat. We relaxed on the hard wooden benches.

The ten o'clock passenger came in on time. We saw several people get off and a couple get on. In a few minutes the train pulled out. Wes and I were depressed that we weren't aboard, but we had decided to save our money and the freight was the way to accomplish that. We accepted our situation and returned to the bench.

"I'm closing up now," the agent announced. "But if you are going to catch the midnight freight I'll leave the waiting room open and the lights on. You don't look like the kind of boys who would make any trouble."

We thanked him with the remaining energy available to us, realizing it was a far cry from the treatment that Shorty Hertz would give us. With that, the agent was gone and we were alone in the waiting room. The demands of the day had been heavy and we were deadly tired. We agreed for one to sleep while the other remained awake and on guard. However, our plan failed as we both fell asleep shortly thereafter.

But before doing so I wondered about the folks back home, about their welfare and realized they had no idea where we were and what we were into. Momentarily pangs of fear and defeat ran through me. "I really feel badly about our retreat to get out of the Badlands. They were hard-fought miles."

"I agree," Wes answered. "Those miles were hard to give up. Another thing that was hard to give up was the passenger train into Rapid City, and for only three dollars apiece. But I agree we just don't have that kind of money."

I let my mind take its own course and found myself saying, "Wes, this trip is like life. We worked hard to get done what we started to do. Some things went well today. We enjoyed them, people treated us well. Some things were not so nice, people didn't treat us well and we were dissatisfied with them, furious at them, wished they weren't so, wished they were different. So we're in this little town, without enough money to ride the passenger train, not enough money to eat in a restaurant or stay in a motel, but we got to keep going."

Wes nodded and I could see he was almost asleep.

Chapter Three
Day Two: Sand Car and Rapid City

We slept deeply for a couple of hours when we were suddenly awakened by screeching wheels and hissing steam from an engine. We jumped to the floor, gathered the luggage and ran out to the depot platform, knowing we had to find a suitable boxcar. Another petroleum car with a catwalk would not do. The engine had moved up the track about fifty yards and began to take on water from a tower there. A stretch of cars was immediately before us and we started toward the engine, hoping to find an open one. We hurried because we saw a brakeman at the other end of the train with a lantern in his hand.

As we reached the puffing engine Wes called out, "Geez, there's not one goddamned open car! Not one!"

"Let's run around in front of the engine and try the other side," I suggested. "We've got to stay away from the brakeman. He's on this side."

We hurried around the throbbing engine, by some good fortune out of the engineer's view. We started searching for a car on that side. We ran quickly with our luggage and soon covered the whole train of cars.

"Gee, we're in trouble. Not a goddamn open car," Wes concluded.

I spied a sand car just as our time was running out. The engine whistle blew and began its huffing and puffing, the exercise it went through before pulling ahead with full steam. I called out, "Let's try this one. We don't have any choice."

"What's inside?" Wes asked.

I shrugged and pulled my luggage up tight. "How do I know?"

The engineer pulled the whistle again. My breathing, which had picked up during our search, was now nearly out of control. Wes nodded his head and climbed the ladder to the top of the car. I followed. He jumped when he reached the top and I heard a thud as he hit an uncertain bottom. It sounded soft like sand.

51

We were lucky. It was sand and the car was filled to four feet from the top. Had it been empty we would have dropped ten feet and hit steel! I followed Wes's jump. Though frightened by dangerous and uncertain prospects, I was relieved that we had found someplace to ride.

Wes laughed. "My God, this is going to be one hell of a ride."

We unwound our shelter halves as the engine began to pick up speed. "This is no Department of Interior national park, but I think we'll get a good night's sleep here," Wes laughed as he pulled the shelter half into position to lie on. He stretched out and I did the same. We looked skyward. The stars were out and a full moon shone brightly. We listened to the clickety clacking of the train wheels as they crossed the point on the rails where one joined the other. We had gotten used to it on our ride on the petroleum car and grown to like it. Indeed, it relaxed us.

"Can't get better than this," Wes exclaimed.

The heavy sleep that encompassed us in the depot soon settled over us again. However, we were awakened several times during the night and felt the train pull onto a siding to allow another train to pass. After a wait we felt the train pull back onto the main tracks and speed onward. It was reassuring to know we were moving west in spite of the delays.

On one of the occasions when I awakened I noticed the stars and moon that had shone brightly earlier were replaced by low hanging dark clouds. I fell back asleep but was awakened soon thereafter by driving rain. I climbed underneath the shelter half, onto the sand, and fell back to sleep. I gave a passing thought to the Badlands, wondering whether we might be passing through the area we had seen that afternoon, or whether we might be beyond that. It all seemed so long ago!

The remainder of the night passed without incident. However, I was startled the following morning by the bright sunshine. I awoke and came out from under the shelter half. Wes was rising at the same time. I saw him pull his trousers off and shake sand from them. I then became aware I had the same problem. Sand had packed itself around my middle, into my shoes and was caked to my head. I looked at Wes and laughed, as his facial expression was distorted by the amount of sand in his hair. He laughed too and pointed at my head, which was also packed with sand. The more we examined each other the more we laughed. "Not as good as home, but this wasn't a bad night's sleep."

After our fun we looked about us. It was the first occasion to see where we had landed and where we had spent the night. At first nothing struck us as unusual. It was huge container on wheels filled with fine sand on its way to someplace unknown to us. The car was scarred by loading equipment that had struck it or failed to place its load accurately. Instead of depositing rocks and gravel in the middle of the car, they may have bounced them off the car's sides.

However, as our eyes scanned the car in detail we were startled to see a large snake, five or six feet long, coiled at the other end of the car. I could see its skin's whole design of big and small brown diamonds set forth in black outlines against a tan background. Its head was heart shaped and dark black. The snake's beady eyes stood out as it surveyed us. Its tongue darted out and in from its menacing, wide-jawed mouth. We were a safe distance from it, yet it looked as if it was ready to strike, though we had not provoked it.

"My God," Wes exclaimed. "Was that damned thing in here all night?"

"Can't be otherwise. There's no way it could have just arrived." My calm was fake. I was as frightened as Wes, maybe more so. "I figure it was very aware of us right from the beginning and moved as far away from us as possible."

"Christ, I can just imagine jumping on it," Wes shouted. "All hell would have broken loose."

Hell was the right thing to say, because Wes would have been bitten for sure and myself as well. I intoned, "We can count our blessings for that not happening. Yes, all hell would have broken loose."

We looked at each other, appreciating our good luck, but in desperation wondering, "What the hell do we do now?"

I observed, "I believe it's a rattler. It's whipping its tail back and forth. Looks just like one and acts like one. The only thing is a rattle at the tip of its tail is missing. Sometimes they lose them. So we have a rattler here even though he doesn't have a rattle, and it's a monster!"

Wes pressed, "So what do we do? We can't ride along with that thing over there! We don't know what it is likely to do!"

Without thinking I suggested, "Why do anything? It hasn't done anything to us yet."

"Yet is right," Wes challenged. "We can't keep it around thinking it will leave us alone. No way."

I thought for a minute and suggested, "Let's take our shelter halves, put them in front of us, like shields, and move on the snake. We should stay several feet apart so the snake has to pay attention to both of us. When we get about three feet or so from the snake, one of us will throw his shelter half over the snake, jump on it and wrap the canvas around it. Then we'll have him!"

"Who's going to do what?" Wes pressed.

"Unless the snake moves toward your shelter half, I'll do the throwing. Let's move so I'll be the closer to him."

"What will we do if it strikes sooner than you throw?"

"If he strikes, I'll throw the shelter half at the same time. It will cover him. He's not going to come three or four feet out of the coil, even if he strikes. If we're careful and smart we should be okay."

"Do you think he might come after me?" Wes asked.

"No more than he will come after me. If he does, just throw your shelter half over him and jump on him."

Wes nodded. "I got it. But what do we do after we've caught him?"

"Bundle him up in the shelter half and throw him over the side."

With our planning completed, we shook the sand out of the shelter halves and started across the car slowly and deliberately. I was sure we were doing the right thing. Yet I continued to wonder if there wasn't something else we could do. The snake watched us come and the two targets confused him. His eyes darted back and forth between the two oncoming canvasses. He tightened his coil and shook the tip of his tail vigorously. He was clearly reacting to our challenge.

I had trouble with my grip on the shelter half because my hands were really sweating and I felt sweat roll down my face. I gripped the shelter half harder and stepped ahead. "Be sure to help me throw him over the side once we get him wrapped up," I ordered, and suggested, "Hold onto the canvas as he flies out into space, like shaking a rug."

Slowly, step by step, step by step, we made our final strides toward the snake, frightened but determined. Its eyes glistened sharply, its tongue worked vigorously and its coil tightened as we got closer and closer.

My heart pounded wildly. I could feel the perspiration running down my back as well as my face. I gripped the shelter half more tightly than ever.

We took one step closer and were about four feet from him. He rose in his coil! A strike was imminent.

I shouted, "Now!" I stepped one pace closer and threw my shelter half over him, jumped on it immediately and wrapped the canvas around him. Wes helped. Quickly we changed the snake into a rounded package and felt him squirm inside the canvas. Though the canvas was scarred from the burning soot of the freight, it was thick enough to keep the snake from biting us.

We carefully carried the bundle to the edge of the car. The snake was moving vigorously and we knew we had to rid ourselves of him quickly. As we approached the side of the car, we raised the bundle over our heads and flipped the canvas over the side of the car as though we were hanging wash out to dry. We snapped the bundle and saw the snake suspended in mid-air for a moment. It fell quickly to the road bed, bouncing on the cinders, lying still for a moment and then moving ever so slowly.

"We did it! We did it! We sacked him and threw him overboard. He really writhed around once the tent was over him, when we wrapped him up!" I, as well as Wes, was almost beside myself. We leaped into the air, fell on the sand and laughed and laughed. "We did it! We did it!" I repeated.

We wondered whether the snake might die but doubted it as the train rolled on. We thought it was just too tough to die.

We talked excitedly about our feat, wiped the perspiration off our faces and hands and wondered again about the kind of snake it was. Wes asked skeptically, "Do you really think it was a rattlesnake?"

"Sure was a rattlesnake, even though it didn't have its rattle," I argued. "I've seen them before."

Wes reasoned, "It was not a bull snake or a black snake. Must have been a rattler unless there is a strange snake in this part of the country that we don't know about."

We celebrated our success with a breakfast of beans and bread. Feeling the special need to celebrate, we splurged and added a can of spaghetti. After leisurely passing the cans back and forth between us and each getting his equal share, we threw the cans over the side of the car with abandon. After ridding ourselves of the snake we were high and needed to show it.

Given our preoccupation with the snake and breakfast, we neglected to view the countryside. We peered over the side of the car, seeing a strange sight. It was desolation in the truest sense. There were no signs of civilization for miles around: no farms, no ranches, no small towns, no fields of grain or corn, just flat desert-like land. The austerity made us feel cozy and safe inside the rolling sand car, especially since we had gotten rid of the snake.

Wes observed, "You know, our burns are healing, but we must brush the sand off of them." With that suggestion we helped each other deal with the problem and applied some more lotion. "Won't be long and we'll be good as new," he concluded.

We walked back to the wall of the sand car to look at the scenery. However, the train slowed and pulled onto a siding. "My God, another one of these," Wes groaned. We withdrew to the center of the car and knelt down quickly when we heard voices.

"I thought I saw a couple kids run around these cars last night about midnight back there in Kadoka. I lost track of them, never saw them again. I sure would like to know what happened to them."

"Hell, they probably are long gone, dropped off someplace during the night. That rain was so hard it wouldn't allow anybody to stay out in it. It was a bad one, all right. But what the hell difference does it make? They couldn't do anything dangerous or harm anything. I figure the highway patrol and our railroad cops keeping hikers off the highway and the railroad cars have gone overboard. There was that one murder, and I agree it was a bad one, but, for Christ's sake, we haven't experienced a crime wave. It was one isolated case."

"Uh huh. Well, let's get back to the caboose and get some coffee. Those kids can take care of themselves, regardless of where they are."

The train pulled back onto the main tracks. About a half hour later we sighted a small town. Its sign read BOX ELDER. We knew we were approaching Rapid City and were disappointed with the engine stopping. We discovered it was to tank up on water and knew the stop would be short.

As we looked over the side of the car we saw a young man approaching. We were sorry that we had shown ourselves. But since we had, we were not going to duck. We stood our ground as he climbed the ladder and jumped in. He was dressed in army clothes and had an officer-type cap. We wondered whether he had been hired from the Army to run down hitchhikers and hobos. Our notion was quickly dispelled as he demanded, "Got anything to eat?"

We shook our heads and responded, "We need something to eat ourselves."

He looked over our suitcases and shelter halves. "I see you are camping. Are you sure you don't have something to eat in those suitcases?" He demanded, "I want to see their insides. I think you are lying!"

Though dressed in a military uniform, he had a shabby, down-at-the-heels kind of a look. Further, we were not in the mood for anyone telling us what to do. In short, we would not be cowed and I announced so with a curt, "No!"

"Besides, who in the hell do you think you are to be telling us what to do?" Wes added with anger.

We were not street fighters but we had been in fights. We turned the tables. We stared him up and down and I challenged, "I don't know why an Army man should be looking for food and why an Army man is looking to ride a freight train, and what's more, either back off or we'll throw you off the train, ass over tea kettle." I was so wrought up that I was seriously tempted to move on him immediately.

He read our stance and backed off. "Right now I'm . . . let's call it over the hill. Not from the Army but a Three-Cs camp—Civilian Conservation Corps. I've done all the shoveling and tree cutting I'm going to do. I am over the hill and glad of it."

He pulled his military cap down his forehead. "I've had it!"

His gesture did not impress us. We judged him weak and trying to cover it with bluff. His sullen face, pronounced jaw and small eyes above his heavy cheekbones didn't fool us. He was weak and vulnerable, and we knew it.

"So they'll be after you?" I conjectured.

"No, they don't fool with runaways. They'll first notify the police and railroad cops to be on the lookout for me. After that, I guess they'll notify my parents and the county office where I enlisted."

Wes and I withdrew to the other side of the car, carrying our things with us. To be sure he didn't see it as fear I said before moving, "You'll have to find your own way, and you better keep your ass on this side of the car."

He read the disdain in my message and lowered his head. We walked away.

The engine pulled away from the water tower, proceeding slowly toward Rapid City. The Conservation Corps runaway kept to himself, saying nothing further. As the train pulled to a stop in Rapid City Wes and I climbed down the ladder with our gear fully intact. I laughed to myself as I saw Wes carrying the wounded suitcase. As we walked out of the railroad yard unmolested by police, we noticed how exceptionally dirty we were. Soot covered our faces, and sand was on our clothes and caked to our scalps, and we still looked like we had measles from the soot burns.

After a thorough cleanup in the railway station, including more lotion for our burns, we walked to the street. Elated and bouncing with excitement, we shouted, "We made it! Rapid City, we are here!"

People passing by looked at us with consternation and amusement. Truly we were a curious sight with our soiled clothes and unusual luggage. We asked a kindly looking man, "Could you tell us where Evans' Service Station is?"

"It's about six blocks away. Go down Fourth Street about four blocks, turn right on Elm for two and you'll find it right on the corner there. You can't miss it."

In our enthusiasm we thanked him profusely and he must have wondered what all that was for.

We hurried to Evans', taking in the full scope of Rapid City as we passed along its streets. A travel agency advertised RAPID CITY: THE COMMERCIAL AND CULTURAL CENTER OF THE BLACK HILLS. Another sign read: ARCHITECTURE AS VARIED AS IT IS OLD—ITALIAN FACADES TO EUROPEAN ONION DOMES.

In less than fifteen minutes we saw Evans' Service Station. It was large and sleek beyond what one would imagine of a service station. Our anxiety built up as we passed by the gas pumps. Much rested on us being able to convince Mr. Evans to let us stay in the athletic dorm. Not only were we unknown to him, but our appearance was ragged.

We entered the station and asked to see Mr. Evans. We tried to be confident but not bold. The attendant ushered us into a large office, exceptional for any business, much less a gasoline station. Somehow it looked like an insurance office. A stately appearing man sat behind a large walnut desk, one covered with models of antique automobiles. He was unusually tall—maybe about six feet four—had a full head of grey hair, a small, well trimmed mustache and intense blue eyes. There was a sternness that came through clearly as he carefully looked us over. Such persons as ourselves were rather unusual for him to see at the beginning of a business day, and yet we felt fairness in his scrutiny.

We awkwardly introduced and explained ourselves, referred to my brother and asked whether we might stay in the downstairs dormitory for several days. I even mentioned plans, though most tentative, to attend the School of Mines.

He commented, "So you're Elmer's brother."

I nodded.

"You sure look alike. I have great respect for him. I hope he returns to the dorm in September. He's bright, decent, responsible and good to have around. You know, he's awfully fast, quick, and was the running back for the Mines last year until he got hurt. He was hobbling around here on crutches for two or three weeks. Had a bad knee. I don't know how he was hurt but I hope he comes back this year to the dorm and to the team. Then he is quite a student too. I think he ended first in his class after the first year."

Mr. Evans paused. "Back to your moving into the dorm—go ahead, use it for a week or ten days." After serious thought he added, "All the boys have gone for the summer, and we were about to clean it for the fall semester. It won't be long and they'll be back, some of the regulars and some new ones." He paused and looked us over carefully again. "We can put off cleaning for a week. That won't make any difference." He continued to look at us, now more critically. "I guess you had a hard trip. You've certainly come a long ways."

He didn't ask about the condition of our clothes or our general appearance. However, we knew he was keenly aware of them. "Why don't you go down to the dorm and get cleaned up. Then come back and see me."

Elated, Wes and I walked down a long stairway. Though well lighted, we were careful. It was new to us. When we reached the bottom of the stairs we discovered the most extraordinary basement. It was about thirty feet wide and ninety feet long, running under the whole length of the station, including its offices, several service areas and room to store tires. The back side had several large windows where the ground dropped away from the building. There was a shower room, a laundry and a line of closets. The beds were bordered by dressers and study tables. So each boy had his own bay area. The basement was painted gold and navy blue, the School of Mines' colors, having a dramatic effect, though it struck us as being "too much."

The final touch of the dramatic setting was a huge portrait of a miner painted on one of the walls. He was full size, wearing a lantern mounted on the bill of his cap and swinging a pick. Underneath the painting was a distinctive inscription: A FIGHTING HARDROCKER.

We did as Mr. Evans instructed and returned to his office thoroughly scrubbed and wearing our change of clean clothes. We also put some of Mr. Jackson's lotion to our burns. It was about ten o'clock. Though we had had a breakfast of sorts, Mr. Evans judged our circumstances. He began, "It's just the start of the day. If you are going sight seeing, it will be a long trek. Now I'd like to get you started right. By that I mean I want to take you to a Rapid City breakfast—one that will get you on your way and keep you fortified all day." He encouraged, "Follow me."

We soon faced an odd-looking car. "This is my Stanley Steamer," Mr. Evans announced proudly. "If you'll get in we'll drive down to Cal's Diner." With smooth but odd chug-chugging and hissing we rode several blocks, pulling up in front of a large diner. We left the car at the curb with a strange light beaming under its engine—a device to keep the steam charged up for our return trip.

We walked through some impressive large doors onto a heavy carpet, all out of character for a diner. It was more upscale. A large, jovial man met us at the entry point. "Ed, you've got a couple of bright boys with you this morning. Maybe a couple of grandsons?"

Mr. Evans laughed. "Not quite, but I do have a couple of fine boys who need two of your super breakfasts."

Soon after being seated we were served orange juice, dry cereal with cream, bacon and eggs, as well as sausage and a side order of potatoes. Though we were not coffee drinkers we gulped a couple of cups with our meal.

In the meantime Mr. Evans listened to our sightseeing interests, commented occasionally and volunteered, "I've got a man delivering some tires to Hot Springs tomorrow. He'll deliver you right to the front of Mt. Rushmore. That's one you won't have to worry about. It's in the immediate area of Mt. Harney. You'll want to see that. It's the highest peak in South Dakota. Don't forget to see the work that is being done on the monument for Crazy Horse. He was an outstanding Sioux chief. It's scheduled to be bigger than the Mt. Rushmore memorial. It's being carved out of mountain granite, just like Rushmore. And try to work in Sylvan Lake and the Wind Cave."

Mr. Evans had a sip of his coffee and continued. "Then, while you are in the south don't overlook Hot Springs. There's more down there than most folks know about. First there are warm, mineral-laden waters. They attract people with all kinds of ailments ranging from rheumatism to emphysema. Now you boys look pretty healthy and don't need all of that, but you might like a quick dip in those waters just for fun. To show you how popular the waters are, the Sioux and Cheyenne Indians fought over them. There is an excavation site near there where as many as a hundred mammoths drank water, all at one time, as long ago as twenty-six thousand years. Also, you'll see hundreds of wild mustangs. They have a sanctuary on a range west of Hot Springs. Finally there are some sandstone buildings that have intricate carvings you'll want to see. So don't miss them."

Mr. Evans expanded. "Up north is still another story, but unless you can handle another breakfast we'll have to cover that at another time. But you'll want to see Sturgis, Deadwood, Lead, Spearfish and Bell Fourche."

We sat back from the breakfast table, satisfied and relaxed.

"You handled all of that food quite well," Mr. Evans noted. We agreed; however, we did not tell him that it was our second breakfast of the day.

"Here is a detailed map of the area," he continued and pressed the map into my hands. "Now, if you figure you don't need any more to eat, we'll go back to the station and you can start your sightseeing right here in Rapid City."

The ride back in the Stanley Steamer was as exciting as our trip to the diner. Mr. Evans left us at the door to the dorm and said, "Stay in touch with me. I want to know where you plan to go."

Wes and I returned to the dormitory, put a load of laundry through the washer and dryer and repacked the suitcases, as we planned to take only one with us, and the pup tent too, on our travels outside Rapid City. Such would not start until tomorrow, but we looked ahead. We were sure to pack the undamaged suitcase, as we planned to use it and leave the other in the dormitory.

With that taken care of, we climbed the stairs with light steps and entered the streets of Rapid City. An attendant at the gas pump suggested, "Whatever you see, be sure to include Dinosaur Park. It's a ways from here, up on Sky Line Drive, but you can walk it. If you'll just follow this street, turn right on Broadway, go about a mile, then you'll run into the Drive. Follow it on out."

We walked through the city lightly, as we were not lugging our baggage. Our experience was limited to Sioux Center, a city of less than a thousand people, and an occasional visit to Yankton, probably something over five thousand. Things here were larger, shinier and faster. We loved it.

When we got to Sky Line Drive our walk became challenging, but we persevered our way up. We stopped to rest after climbing about a mile. We looked back and enjoyed the spectacular view of the city. Finally, after giving the climb our ultimate effort, we made it to the top and were dazzled by a whole park full of life-size dinosaurs. Being made of cement they had withstood the wear of climbing children. Wes exclaimed, "Did you ever imagine seeing such a thing when you were back in Sioux Center, back there sitting on the creek bank?"

"No, no," I laughed. With that we climbed every dinosaur and ancient lizard in sight. "If Mr. Hanson could only see us now! He would say, 'Go for it!' and maybe give us a little lecture on the geology of these animals, if that's what you call that kind of thing—when they lived and what the country was like then."

Exhausted by the mountain and dinosaur climbing, we sat on a wall at the highest point of the park and enjoyed looking out over the city below. We had seen it noted in some brochure, but had forgotten it: that is, a canyon divides Rapid City into east and west. Now, overlooking the city, we could clearly see it. It all was breathtaking.

An Army band appeared as if from nowhere, and as it marched by it struck up the "Stars and Stripes Forever." Our emotions moved up and topped the pleasure of seeing the dinosaurs. "This is really great!" Wes exclaimed. "It just makes you feel like you ought to do something good for somebody!"

I nodded my head, smiled and sensed Wes and I were together on that. We later learned that it was the Rapid City National Guard band on a practice exercise. It seemed like anything but an exercise to us.

We walked down the mountain, marveling at the ease of the journey compared to walking up. We liked the hairpin curves. They gave us a chance to stop and study the country around us. They gave leisure to the hike. On the way up they also had given us a resting place and eased the punishment of the climb. On our current stop we saw free roaming antelope and wild turkeys. Wes whispered, "Let's see how close we can get." With that we left the road, but were only able to advance several steps before the antelope ran off in a lope. We had not threatened them, but they just liked to maintain their distance. The turkeys were a different matter, as we were able to get within ten yards of them before they made an awful gobbling noise and flew off.

"You know, I've not seen either one of those before," I admitted with excitement. "Have you?"

Wes shook his head. "No. I have just heard my dad tell of them. There are some down along the river near Yankton, but none around Sioux Center."

Coming back to town we discovered the School of Mines. It was on our list of things to see, but it was a surprise. We entered the campus and wandered in and out of several buildings which were classrooms and faculty offices. Luckily, we came across the Museum of Geology. We spent the next hour and a half studying the exhibits of fossils, remains of plant and animal life of previous geological periods. Though currently in the form of a rock or mineral, the fossils initially were plants and animals. Many different minerals were shown, all with strange names attached to them. We moved from display to display and our breath was taken away by the scope of life they presented in earlier periods. We had no idea that such things existed, or that the earth had a history extending over billions of years. To see this immediately before me fired my imagination.

"Isn't this great!" Wes exclaimed.

I nodded in disbelief of what I was seeing. My hope to become a geologist was touched and I was determined to improve my grades in science and math, as they were the key to becoming a geologist and coming to the School of Mines.

We discovered a bench as we left the museum. "Geez, am I glad to sit down. This damned walking is getting me down. It's harder than hitchhiking," Wes grumbled.

"Really?" I asked.

"Not really," Wes came back. "What did you think of the dinosaur park? Of the museum?"

"I'll never forget them. Never saw anything like them. Never saw anything with so much thought mixed in, running all the way through them, you know, the exhibits. Never." I laughed. "On just the park, not the museum, I can see Alley Oop and Denny the Dinosaur hanging out in one of the prehistoric swamps!"

"On the museum, did it encourage you to try for the School of Mines?" Wes asked. He pushed further. "So, are you ready to enroll?"

"It looks okay, but you can't tell the whole story from what we've seen. The campus is okay, and the school has a great reputation. It's the teaching and academics that give the school its recognition. We couldn't see any of that, but I'm sure they are here. My brother told me all about them, especially how the professors know their stuff and are tough on the students. And he told me that lots of companies come to interview the graduates for jobs, not just mining companies."

"You haven't said whether you are ready to take that on."

"I'll see," I said simply and said no more.

Wes nodded and suggested, "You know, it's about two o'clock and we haven't had lunch."

"Don't need it," I responded. "We had two breakfasts. The one with Mr. Evans was out of this world!"

"I agree, we don't need it," Wes pleaded, "but I still would like lunch. I'm used to it."

Wes gave up the idea of lunch and we walked back to the dorm feeling like we were really learning our way around. When we entered the station, we talked to the attendants and reported our experience to Mr. Evans.

"Great," he said. "You boys are doing it right. I'm pleased with the way you go after it. Now, in connection with your plans tomorrow, as I said earlier I have a young man, Otto Hoffer, making a run south. There will be plenty of room in the cab of the truck for both of you. I'll have him get in touch with you and you can see that part of the Hills."

We thanked him and returned to the dorm.

Though we had spent less than a couple hours in the dorm, we felt very much at home there. Wes pulled a large can of spaghetti from his suitcase, added peaches and bread. After opening the cans we passed them back and forth between us, starting with the spaghetti and following with the peaches and bread. "This is a little early for supper," Wes reasoned, "but I am hungry."

"What a day," I said while eating.

"It really was great. It's hard to imagine we were on a freight this morning, fending off a bum runaway from a CCC camp."

"And fighting a snake," I added.

Afterwards we went back on the street, walked around, window-shopped and observed the activity around the restaurants and bars. Other than the sparkle of the lights there was not much for us to see.

We returned to the service station, where one of the attendants approached us. "Mr. Evans said you want to go south to see Mt. Rushmore and other sights. I leave here at seven-thirty and will take you right to those places. I will probably get you there before the places open."

We were happy with this invitation and replied with an enthusiastic, "Yes!"

"I'll tell the fellow who opens the station. He'll wake you at six-thirty. Incidently, my name is Otto Hoffer. Get a good night's rest. I'll see you in the morning." Before he broke away we introduced ourselves, and we felt Otto would be good company.

We walked to the dorm, enjoyed a good hot shower, realizing it might be our last one for several days. I took a long look at the HARDROCKER before turning the light off. He seemed almost real, staying imprinted on my mind as I fell asleep. Indeed, he helped rid my mind of the snake.

Chapter Four
Day Three: Mt. Rushmore and More

We were wakened at six-thirty and hurried to get ready for the day. Though we didn't like it, we had a can of spaghetti for breakfast, had a big drink of water, closed the suitcase, each picking up half of the pup tent and trudged up the stairs. I carried the only suitcase.

"You're early," Otto noted. "But since you're ready, why don't we leave."

We climbed in the cab of a sizable truck loaded with tires. We threw our baggage in back and with the usual grinding of gears we were off.

Otto was very open and began, "Mr. Evans is a great guy. I used to live in the dorm, went to Mines, played football but flunked out. He gave me this job. I've had to work, and work hard. But I would not have the job if it wasn't for him. I've gotten it together since I flunked out. So come September I am going back to become an electrical engineer. Football was mad. So I've dropped that. I'll stay in the dorm. Mr. Evans has a little job for me. I'll get along okay."

We passed through the city as Otto talked, and we were presently on the outskirts of town. "There's a lot of stuff that has grown up to attract the tourists. You can see the wildlife parks, water parks, amusement parks, trail rides and an aircraft museum. But you're on the way to see the bigger and better things."

He asked about our plans and urged, "You ought to go on into Wyoming and see what's there, even go on up to see Glacier National Park in Montana. You'll never see a more grand sight than Glacier National Park!"

We listened politely and suggested that we would come back for that at another time. "It's just a little too much for us right now," I explained.

Otto was not put down and encouraged, "Think it over. Don't rule it out. You may never make it back out here again. You are just at the right jumping off place to do it."

We nodded our heads but made no further comment.

He continued, but now in a different way. "I can give you time to get a full look at Rushmore, and unless you want to spend time there, I'll run you over to see the Custer Game Park and Sylvan Lake. We can do all of that and I can still make my run down to Hot Springs on schedule."

"Sounds great," was Wes's response and I agreed, but asked, "Would we miss anything?"

"Yes, you would miss the Wind Cave, which is a big thing with some people."

'What makes it great?" I asked.

"It's the eighth longest cave in the world. It has seventy-six miles of passageways with box work, frost work and popcorn crystals. Above ground is a twenty-eight thousand-acre wildlife park featuring bison, longhorn sheep and prairie dogs. It's just ten or twenty miles north of Hot Springs. I could drop you off there and you could check all that out. I will go on and you can hitch it from there."

I looked at Wes and he seemed in agreement with the plan. "Okay," I said. "Let's do it."

Otto was a master at wheeling the truck around. We took the pigtail curves, steep climbs, sharp curves and rapid declines with ease and excitement. He didn't speak as he accomplished these feats, but frowned with determination. He broke his silence as we started through a tunnel and shouted, "There they are, all four presidents! They are framed by the borders of the tunnel. You can see that yourselves!"

Wes and I were amazed and startled by the hugeness of the whole memorial and the individual faces of the presidents. "Yes! Yes!" we shouted back to Otto.

Otto smiled and slowed the truck so the view would be continued as long as possible. We finally passed through the tunnel, and though the drama of the frame was lost, the immensity of the four presidents was even greater than before and we could see them very clearly now.

Otto continued his role as tourist guide. "Mt. Rushmore is a memorial to four great Americans—Washington, Jefferson, Lincoln and Theodore Roosevelt. The mountain has the largest figures of any statues in the world! Alone, the head of Washington is as high as a five-story building. The height of the head is to the scale of a human being four hundred sixty-five feet tall. The memorial was begun in 1927 and continued, with some lapses, for over fourteen years. Gutzon Borglum designed it and supervised most of the work."

Otto stopped talking, took a turn in the road and announced, "Here we are!"

In the best government sign-making possible a sign read: MT. RUSHMORE MEMORIAL PARK.

Otto directed, "Why don't you get out and look around for about fifteen minutes. I'll wait for you and after you come back I'll drive on."

Wes and I did exactly that and caught the huge size and wonder of the memorial. The four presidents' faces stared out across the canyon. Yet we felt as if they were looking directly at us. There were only a few people there at that early hour so we imagined the sight was just for us. When the allotted time was over we raced back to the truck, exclaiming about the spectacular view and thanking Otto for waiting. We would have liked to have stayed longer but appreciated Otto's special consideration.

"Mr. Evans likes you fellows and I know he wouldn't mind me doing this. We have traveled less than thirty miles and only about half hour has been spent. I'll swing over to Highway 86 so you can see the Game Lodge. It's about five miles. I'll drive by the lodge slowly so you can get a full view of it. I don't have to get to Hot Springs before ten o'clock."

"What's the Game Lodge known for?" I asked.

"Sometimes people speak of it as the Summer White House. That's because President Coolidge spent a summer there. Many fines rooms in there, fabulous, including a terrific dining room with some special name, I think 'The Pheasant Room', and of course, a lounge. It's like a hotel."

I asked, "How do you know all these things?"

Otto chuckled. "I worked as a tour bus driver for a couple of summers when I first came out here from Ohio. I had to learn these things so I could describe them to the tourists. It was a terrific job, lots of fun; however, I had to get something regular." He shifted his tone. "There are over seventy-three thousand acres in this park. I'm sure we'll see some buffalo on our way out."

Sure enough, as we drove out of the park we saw a large herd. "My God! They are big!" Wes exclaimed. Although I said nothing I was of the same mind.

"Wasn't that Game Lodge a wonderful old building?" Otto noted. "With the stone facing and all, I can see why a president would choose it. I'm surprised more haven't come, but they haven't. Now, before we leave this area I'm showing you Sylvan Lake. I'm sure you've heard about it, and if you haven't, you will. It's just up the road a short way."

It appeared shortly. Nestled below needle-pointed spires, its blue water stretched for some distance to a sandy swimming beach. "Too bad we don't have more time. A swim would be great," I remarked.

Otto nodded and followed with, "I'll swing over to Highway 36 so you can see some other things. Harney Peak is next on our way. I'll swing north on the highway about five miles so you can see it. Then I'll turn around and head back south on 89. I'll point it out. It's the tallest mountain east of the Rockies."

In a matter of fifteen minutes Otto exclaimed, "There she is, over there to your left!"

Even if we hadn't gotten the personal direction we would have known the peak was something special, it was so high, so impressive and majestic. Both Wes and I shook our heads in wonder.

Otto was not a slow driver, and he turned the truck around headed south, trying to make up for lost time. The speed was exhilarating. Besides, the trip was beyond all of our fantasies. The scenery along the way was breathtaking, and added to the speed of the truck, pushed our emotions to an all-time high.

"There are the Needles over there," Otto pointed out. "As you can see, they are tall, thin and they are all rock. That's why they are called the Needles." He continued, "We'll soon get to the town of Custer. The town's name commemorates the General who first led an expedition of twelve hundred men into this area in 1874. He was ordered here to investigate the threat of the Indians, not to fight. Maybe they were trying to scare the Indians, so they sent that many men. It was later, in 1876, that he made his last stand at Little Big Horn and was massacred. He completely misjudged the strength and strategy of the Indians and was done in by his mistake. The General was a wild character, but he described the splendor of the area in his journal and did it much better than I am doing."

Otto added, "Probably more important was the first discovery of gold in the Black Hills made on French Creek, east of Custer. A member of Custer's expedition confirmed the rumors of the precious metal's existence when he found gold while panning in the creek."

Though Otto slowed as we passed through Custer, he still exceeded the speed limit by considerably more than the allowed thirty miles an hour. We rode on about ten miles, coming to Pringle, a small western town. "I've been so busy doing my tour director's job that I have forgotten to ask about your brother Elmer," Otto apologized. "How is he? Where is he? And is he coming back to Mines and the dorm?"

"Let's see," I said, trying to organize my answer. "He's okay as far as I know. He's in North Dakota working on a farm. Yes, he plans to come back to Mines, but I don't know about the dorm. He's not going to play football any more, so he won't be eligible for the dorm."

"Good. Good," Otto replied. "On the dorm, Mr. Evans might make an exception. He did for me. Elmer shouldn't give up on that."

"I know he plans to ask."

Otto nodded. "He's a smart fellow. He was a freshman and I was a junior. Yet he was helping me with one of my tougher courses, the Theory of Numbers. I would never have made it without his help." He paused and laughed. "If he comes back to the dorm he might get me through another course!"

Otto shifted his tone. "Well, fellows, I am going to drop you off at the Wind Cave in a few minutes. I hope you've enjoyed your trip. Be careful. I'll see you when you get back to the Evans' dorm." He stopped at an impressive government sign. We thanked him and pulled our luggage from the truck. In a moment Otto drove away at a speed that meant he was making up lost time.

Wes looked at his watch. "It's just ten-thirty. What a trip. What timing! We're going to go a long way today, I can feel it."

"And no chicken shit ride!" I exclaimed.

"Yeah, yeah," Wes laughed. "I can still smell it!"

We knew sightseeing would cost us. So we each gave up two dollars as we passed into the entrance of the Wind Cave. Having seen so many things without charge made us feel ready to pay the two dollars admission.

There were about a dozen people waiting for the tour and we joined them. The guide, a woman dressed in a smart dark green uniform with an emblem of the U.S. Park Service on her hat and the lapels of her coat, stood at near attention as we milled around. She looked sharp, like the best of the military. We were impressed and followed her as if she were the leader of a platoon of soldiers. She announced in a formal voice, "This cave, Wind Cave, is the eighth longest in the world." It was just as Otto had explained it, including the stalactites hanging from the vaulted ceiling and the stalagmites standing in opposition on the floor. There were crystal formations overhead and various kinds of colored stone lining each side of the passageway.

We walked several miles on our tour, at first deeply into the cave, then evenly along what seemed to be the bottom of the cave, though there may have been another deeper passage below it. It was during this deeper part of the tour that the full impact of the formations struck me. They weren't different from what we had seen, but they were bigger and there were more of them. I looked in awe and heard our fellow tourists sigh and exclaim.

We finally started climbing to the top. All the while the wind blew around us. It was cooler than a Dakota summer. We reasoned that the wind was caused by the pressure brought about by the drop of the passageways from the surface above. We never understood it, but it added to the excitement of the place.

"Worth every cent of the two dollars," Wes evaluated as we came to the surface about an hour after entering.

I agreed. But for some strange reason I had second thoughts about spending the two dollars. It was money well spent but I worried about covering our expenses on the rest of the trip, especially the unknowns.

Upon returning to the surface we claimed our luggage left with the guard. He had been reluctant to accept it but was pleasant when we retrieved the stuff. We looked around about an hour, watching a herd of buffalo and a flock of wild turkeys. We were in a picnic area and Wes pulled a can each of beans and spaghetti from the suitcase. We ate them without hesitation and were pleased with the menu. Though our table manners left much to be desired, our routine of passing the cans back and forth between us worked well.

We sat for a while, feeling unhurried, and marveled at the cave and the other things we had seen. "Quite a morning! Quite a morning," I said with the full feelings of a new, inexperienced traveler.

Wes continued the gushing. "And all were packed together so closely. Thanks to Otto."

I added, "Yes, yes. And to Mr. Evans."

"Well, let's go on and see Hot Springs. Other than being about ten miles south of here and about fifty miles south of Mt. Rushmore, there's not much I can say. I suppose they have great swimming, golfing and hiking there, but we're not doing any of those."

"Don't forget hot baths. They are supposed to soak away your aches and headaches along with your worries too. I read about them in the stuff Mr. Evans gave us."

We walked out to Highway 305, put our luggage down and thumbed the first car that came down the road. Low and behold, it stopped! It was so out of character with our previous experience that we were shocked.

An appealing, kind man greeted us with a note of optimism. "You fellows look like you're trying to get to Hot Springs." We agreed. His welcome was, "Get in and we'll get underway."

We were no more than seated when he asked, "Are you coming home?"

"No. No," I answered. "We're sightseeing."

"Well, I don't suppose the Chamber of Commerce would like me to say this, but if you've seen the Wind Cave you've about seen what there is to see down here." He paused and corrected himself. "I take that back. There are some giant sandstone block buildings that you should see." He paused again and observed, "I figure you probably need transportation to see them, so I'll fix you up with that. It won't take long and the buildings are worthwhile."

He paused and looked us over. "You fellows may be a little young for moving around the country like you're doing. A little young, yes. Where are you from? And what are your names?"

I answered matter-of-factly, "Sioux Center. I'm Carl and this is Wes."

"Sioux Center, that's way across the state. You boys are a long, long way from home."

We agreed. The man exuded friendliness and good will. "Well, you're very welcome out here in what some people call the 'real west'. You sure are. Now, where else do you plan to go next?"

"After we leave Hot Springs we're going north to see more of the Black Hills and the towns up there: Bell Fourche, Lead, Deadwood and Spearfish."

"More power to you. You'll find all that worthwhile. Where do you plan to sleep along the way?"

We pointed to the pup tent on the floor of the car.

"Hmm. I see you aren't against roughing it. I should have told you, my name is Bill Neal. I grew up right here in Hot Springs. Lived my whole life here. Travel for a living. I sell auto parts. Keeps me busy. Sure does."

We nodded as he drove into Hot Springs.

"The buildings I'm going to show you were taken apart piece by piece about forty or fifty years ago, packed and moved up here from about ten or twelve miles south. That's where they used to be. They have become the center of the banking district.

You can see them right over there—mostly sandstone and all. Pretty impressive, I'd say."

He drove us by the buildings several times, then drove us by several beautiful parks and proudly announced, "That ends my tour. I'll take you back to the edge of town so that you can start north. Unless you fellows want to stop and take a hot bath."

"We had planned to see some of the houses that are talked about, Victorian houses. Ones with fancy woodwork on them," I suggested. "Could you tell us where they are? We can walk it and won't take any more of your time."

"I plumb forgot about them. We're right near them, so I'll give you a closeup look right from the car. Won't take long." Mr. Neal turned his car at the next corner and in a few minutes we were in a distinctive neighborhood of old, well maintained Victorian houses. As we were still appreciating them, Mr. Neal asked, "Now, is there anything else?"

"You've done enough. Might you drop us here? We'll wander through the neighborhood to get a good feel for it. Then we'll walk to the edge of town."

"Sure about that?" Mr. Neal asked. "That baggage you're carrying around looks heavy and clumsy. I'll run you by once more. You can drink them all in. Then I'll run you to the edge of town. All in all, it will save you time. Believe me, I know. I once did a little hitchhiking. Not like you're doing but I did enough of it to know its problems."

We accepted Mr. Neal's offer, sat back and appreciated the beauty of the houses. Though we liked what Mr. Neal was doing for us we were uncomfortable, feeling he was doing too much. After we had seen the houses again, Mr. Neal drove us to the edge of town. He dropped us off with the final remark, "Sure admire your spunk, and good luck to you."

We took our luggage out of his car, thanked him and he was gone.

Wes pulled the map of South Dakota out of his pocket. It was the one given to us by the attendant at the Texaco station in Sioux Center. After a quick look Wes suggested, "Let's try for Newcastle, Wyoming. That's on the way to Spearfish and Belle

Fourche. It's just a little west of South Dakota. The highway takes us right through there."

"Great," I said, feeling we were on a roll and ought to keep going. As we shuffled about positioning ourselves at the edge of the road I spoke about one part of the people's behavior, that is, those people who picked us up. "They surely look us over and sooner or later, usually sooner, want to know where we are going and where we are from, and they like to know our names. Usually, but not always, they give their names and say something about themselves."

I continued to think about it. "I guess its the thing to expect. It's not quite like being in a formal receiving line, like at a Boy Scout dinner or a wedding. But almost. It's just something people do to make contact and carry on a conversation or an activity."

Wes smiled slyly. "Now you sound like you are making a report to Mr. Hanson's civics class on something fancy that he calls social relations!"

I agreed and turned my attention to hitchhiking.

Almost immediately a middle-aged man pulled alongside, asking us the usual questions. When satisfied with our answers he said, "I'm going to Spearfish by the way of Newcastle. As long as you boys are looking around this part of the country, you may like that run."

The man spoke in an easy drawl, western-like. It fit in with his sombrero tipped back smartly on his head. His skin was leathery tan and his eyes were a clear blue and friendly. He appeared to be about fifty.

He continued, "The whole run will take about an hour and a half."

We did some quick arithmetic. We could be in Spearfish as early as mid- afternoon—time to do some sightseeing and find a campsite. We jumped in at his invitation. I sat up front and Wes hauled our luggage into the back seat with him.

"I'm Tex Webster. Been in these parts a long time. No better country than this right through here."

We agreed but did not say anything. The way we were being treated made us feel very good about the whole area.

The beauty of the Black Hills continued to stand out as we rode along, sharper than it had in Hot Springs. The sage brush, which we were expecting, made its appearance and as we drove west it got thicker. As Newcastle appeared on the horizon, Tex Webster, who had been humming to himself, said, "It's a friendly place; got a small museum that tells about the early days. A lot of people stop in there on the way to Devil's Tower. That's out in Wyoming about fifty miles. Worth seeing but we won't pass it on this trip."

We were tired but hadn't been aware of it. Now, as I realized we had hardly spoken, I tried to be good company. After all, Mr. Webster was giving us a ride. "Have you seen Devil's Tower?" I asked.

"Oh, yes. Many times."

"Why do they call it Devil's Tower?"

"Well, I don't have the full story, or I should say myth, because it isn't true, but a long time ago some Indian climbed up there to escape a bear. It was a plain butte then, but the bear clawed up the butte something ferocious, reached all the way to the top but slid down, leaving his claw marks on the sides of the butte. That's how the butte got its furrows. But how it got the name Devil's Tower, I just don't know." Tex Webster sat back from the steering gear and chuckled. He slowed to pass through Newcastle. "Boys, that's it. You better look fast or you'll miss it."

We did, and saw it was the type of small town that we had gotten used to calling western because the stores had false fronts and often had wooden awnings built out over the sidewalk.

"I've never done business here," Tex Webster observed. "But I understand it's a good town, at least for ranchers. You can get about anything you need here, especially repair parts for your machinery."

After passing through Newcastle we traveled east back to South Dakota, and then turned north toward Spearfish. "Your traveling has a lot of courage to it," Tex Webster observed. "First you had to have courage to get out on the road. Second, you needed courage to keep going. Third, you need it to protect yourselves against shady characters and fourth, you need it to protect yourselves against the cops. It shouldn't be that way, but it is—that is, that you must protect yourselves against the cops. Sure, there was that murder a while back by a hitchhiker. Now the cops want to give fellows like yourselves a hard time, even if you don't have any evil intent."

I nodded and he kept talking. He pushed back in his seat and loosened his grip on the steering wheel. "Boys, on cops I'll tell you how it used to be and I figure it still is, and not just in the bigger places. You have to take it from me for your own protection. I was on the road riding the freights for two seasons when I was young. I followed the harvest through the Dakotas and went onto Canada, up past Winnipeg, mostly shocking and threshing grain. That was in the days before the combine. Yup, followed the harvest riding the freights. After that, I turned west, doing whatever I could find—harvesting beets, helping on small cattle roundups, hauling hay, fixing fences, whatever there was to do. By the time I hit the state of Washington I was worn out, counted my earnings and turned back home to the ranch down at Hot Springs."

Tex thought a moment and continued. "I always stayed away from the railroad police and local cops too. It was hard to know what they might do. You couldn't predict them, but for sure they made trouble. The cops didn't want you hanging out in their towns, and the railroad people didn't want you riding their cars. I didn't have breaking sealed cars in mind, stealing and that kind of stuff, but they didn't know that and didn't care. They weren't particular how they handled me, and weren't bashful about using their clubs. The local police didn't mind your being on the cars, as long as they were sure you hadn't pulled some local job and were hurrying out of town. If they were suspicious they'd pull you off, like they did me once, charged me with vagrancy and held me until they were sure I was clean. Then they threatened to keep me locked up unless I got out of town directly, and the freight was the best way of doing that."

Tex's easy way turned to anger as he talked, and we felt it was real. Though long ago, the experience was very alive. He turned in his seat and faced us. "The reason for telling you this story is to caution you about the highway patrol. They are after anybody who hitchhikes. So take care."

I felt lucky because we hadn't seen a patrolman on our whole trip, but feared that would change and wondered how we might handle it.

Tex drifted into aspects of his early life. "I've spent my whole life out here, like my Dad did before me. I worked right along with him when I was a kid, right up through high school. That's when I took to the road for a couple of summers. After I got that traveling out of my system, I settled down and my dad worked me into running the ranch. A couple years of that training was solid, so he put me in charge of the ranch."

Tex chuckled. "Got a lot of work that still needs doing this summer and early fall." He rubbed his jaw and suggested, "Why don't you come work with me for a couple months. You'd only miss a bit of school. You'd make sixty dollars each—a dollar a day cash and room and board. You wouldn't have any trouble catching up with your schooling when you got back. Not the way I figure it. You're bright boys."

We liked being wanted, even though we knew it wasn't possible. On the other hand, we liked school and didn't want to miss it. Besides, we aimed to make the football team. If we stayed two months, the football season would be over by the time we got back.

When we failed to answer right away, Tex talked further. "The work will be hard, but not miserable. I got to rebuild my feeding lot, fix some fence and get ready for winter. Beside the work, I expect you boys would be interested in two or three girls in the neighborhood, just your age—pretty, too. There's a dance every Saturday night, and I'm sure they would be over to my place to borrow something just as soon as they learned of your being there. You know, to make your acquaintance. And if they didn't do that I'd go over and see them to see what's the matter, learn whether they knew you were with me. No matter what, I'd arrange things if it got to that. You can count on it. I know you'd have a good time!"

I suspected that Wes, like me, was enjoying the possibility of meeting the girls, almost getting carried away with it, letting it fog our better judgment. But somehow I got the courage to refuse his generous gesture. But it took some time for me to clear my mind.

"I can see you boys have chosen the important thing, education. I've got a boy up at Spearfish just finished his second year. He's decided to be an engineer. So he's transferring to the School of Mines this fall. As a matter of fact, in a couple of weeks I'm going up to take him home on this very trip. He's been in Spearfish this summer taking some extra work."

The hills grew taller and more rugged as we drove north. The sage brush, which was so prominent earlier, dropped out, replaced by green-blackish pine trees. Tex's easy manner and the serene landscape relaxed us.

However, our pulses quickened when we arrived in Spearfish. It was neat, clean and well groomed and looked like the people had money to spend on nice houses and good streets. Tex drove directly to the teachers' college. It was five- thirty p.m. now. "Leave your gear in the car. Let's find Todd. He's up in this building, Turner Hall."

When we reached room 225, Tex knocked but did not wait for an answer. Instead, he walked in and beckoned us to follow. Immediately an exclamation rang out. "Hi, Dad. I figured you were due about now!"

A quick embrace followed and Tex picked up, "These are a couple of adventurers I picked up down at Hot Springs. I tried to make them into cowboys for a couple of months, but didn't have any luck. Not even after I told them about the side benefits of the job, the beauties in the neighborhood."

Todd played along with the joshing. "That's because they never saw them, or had a chance to check them out." He continued, "More important for the moment is to show the boys around, and after a fifteen minute tour we'll stop in the cafeteria. It's a little early in the day, but since the kitchen staff will be closing the place down, they'll be glad to see us, just to get rid of us. It's the last meal of the summer."

We passed through the food line and with Todd's encouragement filled our plates to the brim and added side dishes. As we finished our meal, Todd asked, "Where do you plan to spend the night?"

"Camping," I replied. "There must be a municipal park in town. Might you tell us where it is?"

"No need to do that," Todd answered. "Stay in my room tonight. There are two beds in the room. I'll talk to the dorm counselor. I know he'll give his okay. I may have to tell him you are a couple of prospective students looking over the school. That will be sure to do it. All you need are two sets of sheets. I'm sure he'll issue them to you."

Regretfully that ended our contact with the Websters, Tex and Todd. We shook hands with them before they left, thanking them for their generosity. We pulled our luggage from the car. As Mr. Webster drove away, he suggested, "If you ever want to be cowboys, even for a short time, get in touch with me!"

I knew we had made right decision in turning down the ranching job. It was done for objective reasons. In another way of looking at it, I figured it would be hard to break away after spending two months with Tex. He was a contagious person. Besides, we really needed an education.

We were sorry to see them leave. However, we were elated with the prospect of a secure, comfortable night's rest in the dormitory. Todd had spoken to the counselor and he came by with two sets of sheets. "Todd told me you would be spending the night here. I'm in a hurry, but I want to welcome you and I hope you decide to enroll. It's a great school."

"Thanks," both Wes and I offered, and before we could say anything else the counselor was gone.

After showering we lay on our beds reading copies of the college newspaper. When we turned out the lights Wes said, "If Dan Larson could only see us now he would be proud of us! We are really fulfilling his dream of our being in his beloved college, and living in comfort."

Chapter Five
Day Four: We Leave College

We took advantage of the comfortable beds and slept in. We didn't leave the dorm until ten o'clock. Unable to find the counselor to thank him, we left him a note. The place was deserted. We were the last to leave.

We looked around the campus, noting its beauty. However, we did not follow Dan's advice and call on the coach. Our college plans, while unorganized, looked to the School of Mines and toward colleges in the eastern part of the state. Those were schools we were used to. Our teachers had gone to them and members of our families as well.

We walked about town, more relaxed than we had been during the whole trip. We had been treated exceptionally well, beyond our greatest hopes, and we had no immediate schedule to meet.

We shared carrying the suitcase but it was burdensome nevertheless, especially when added to the weight of a shelter half. We found a bench along the road, and appreciated the relief it gave us, including our aching feet. Wes pulled the map from his pocket and studied it for several minutes, especially the sightseeing information. "Besides the college the main thing I get from this is there is a very different kind of a fish hatchery here—one that you see through glass—a museum, and a terrific scenic drive about twenty minutes north of here, called Spearfish Canyon. Besides, there is a Passion Play here that's gotten national recognition, but it's not playing now."

"Let's go for the museum and then head out for the scenic canyon. Do you figure a road runs through it?"

"Okay, I like that schedule. Yes, there's a highway that goes through the canyon, and it's on the way to Belle Fourche. Just the name of that town—Belle Fourche—has got to make it good."

"The fish hatchery must be different, really different from the one in Sioux Center. Remember when the game warden caught us swimming there and damn near blew his top? I don't know why he should have been so mad. If it weren't for the likes of us causing trouble he wouldn't have a job. They'd phase him out."

"Yes, I remember. But let's skip this one. We won't be able to swim in it."

We laughed, rose from the bench and I remarked, "Let's find the museum."

Admission turned out to be free. We left our baggage at the admission desk and wandered the aisles of the exhibits for about an hour. It was interesting to learn about the area's history, but our feet began to hurt and Wes suggested, "We need some lunch before we strike out for the canyon and Belle Fourche."

We left the museum at twelve o'clock, found a bench nearby to eat our staples of beans and bread. "You know, we missed breakfast today," Wes commented.

I returned, "We didn't need any after the meal last night."

Wes nodded. "Now we are back to beans. They are good, but grim."

"I'm sure glad you brought them, Wes. You know you brought more of the food than I did. I appreciate it."

Wes smiled. "It's okay. My dad picks these up by the case, so it was just a matter of going to the basement to get them. I didn't tell him or my mother. You know, they never would have let me go on this trip if they had known about it. But, just on the food alone, not counting the trip, I'm sure they'd be glad to let us have it."

I nodded my head in thanks.

Wes declared, "The road ahead is the one we want, Highway 85. I hope we get a ride soon. Our luck has been so good. I don't know if I can stand having to hang out on the road hour after hour, wondering whether anybody will pick us up."

I agreed. "It's tough thumbing when car after car pass by us. It gets me down. You know, it makes me feel badly. It's like nobody likes us, wants any part of us."

Wes, who was usually upbeat, let go. "It makes you wonder whether we'll ever get picked up, whether we'll still be here come nightfall. Like we were in the Bad Lands. Makes you worry about everything, even where we'll spend the night."

I reassured, "We've got our pup tent, for insurance."

Wes countered, "But there's always the question, where can we pitch it? Can't just pitch it in the ditch by the side of the road!"

I was optimistic. "Our luck ever since we got out of the bottom of the Badlands has been good. Well, the freight wasn't too good when you figure in the snake, the sand, the rain and the runaway bum at the end of the ride." I paused a moment and continued my recollections. "But ever since we got to Rapid City things have really looked up!"

Wes nodded. "They sure have. You know, we haven't used the pup tent excepting the night in the sand car, but I figure we'll put it up tonight. I don't see any other possibility. There isn't a Spearfish College in every town." Wes paused and added, "I should have given credit to the shelter halves for protecting us from the sparks, soot and cinders and for giving us something to bundle and get rid of the snake!" He laughed as he mentioned the sparks and the snake. "So it's been worth carrying."

I thought about it for a moment and said, "I bet Clarence never thought his Dad's pup tent would see all this use after it had been in his garage for years, ever since World War I. You know, Clarence is really a nice fellow, friendly and all. And he lives in about the best house in town. His father is the doctor and mayor. You know, everyone looks up to him. His mother is refined and all. Clarence has better clothes than anybody. So he's really got it good." I paused and after giving Clarence a second thought added, "But you know, Clarence has it hard. They are so strict with him. He can't run around town like we do. He can't go out to the fish hatchery or the lake. He probably won't even be able to go out for football—at least he hasn't yet."

Wes nodded. "Yeah. I don't think his folks even know he lent us the tent. Since they never use it, they'll never know. But that's not the idea I'm trying to make. What I'm trying to say is they supervise him so closely he doesn't have a chance to make it on his own." I added, "But he's a nice fellow."

"That's not the point," Wes argued. "It's that he doesn't have any real freedom."

I nodded and thought about what Wes had said.

We reached the edge of Spearfish, put the luggage down and took our usual stance for thumbing, Wes out front with his engaging smile and me behind him with our luggage in the background.

"Here comes a strange looking panel truck and he's slowing down," Wes exclaimed.

It stopped and a friendly, elderly man stuck his head out the window. "Can I trust you fellows?"

"Sure," was our quick answer. "We wouldn't hurt anybody."

"Get over here so I can see you eyeball to eyeball."

We crossed the middle of the road and faced the man behind the steering wheel. He sized us up as if we were in a police lineup. When he was satisfied he asked, "Where you headed?"

"Belle Fourche."

"That's where I'm going, and if I can trust you boys not to hurt me, I'll welcome you aboard. But I want to give you fair warning. If you try to hurt me in any way, you can figure on one hell of a time because I have something in store for you, and let me tell you, it will surprise you. If you try to hurt me you'll be stumbling around without your heads!"

We pleaded our innocence again, and the driver responded, "Okay. Get in but just remember what I told you."

We had no doubt that he was referring to a gun he carried. Yet we were not afraid. He was friendly, straightforward, just protecting his interests.

"I didn't get your names and I forgot to tell you mine. I'm Ted Sloan and I sell tobacco. You must have seen the sign 'GRANGER' painted on the side panel of my truck. That's who I work for. A small company, but a good one. I've got about three more years to go until I retire. I don't know what I'll do then, but I'm sure I'll miss being with Granger."

After this long introduction we completed introducing ourselves. "I'm Carl and this is Wes."

Following this an active conversation began. Mr. Sloan told about his trade territory, how he got into business thirty years earlier, his work over the years, his planned retirement, "right here in the Hills." He included his war experiences. "Yes, it was one foggy morning. We knew the Germans would come at us, but we didn't expect a major assault and one with so much firepower. But it was awful, especially the noise, the smoke, the confusion, the yelling and screaming of the wounded on both sides."

Fear froze us as we were captivated by Mr. Sloan. We sat on the fronts of our seats like we were at a war movie in which the hero was about to be destroyed. Mr. Sloan was so engrossed, so overwrought, he shouted. "What I've said is awful, God-awful, but I've sidestepped the real horror, and that was the killing. There were bodies falling on both sides of me. I didn't know what the hell to do. I felt like I was going to piss in my pants. But I just kept firing and firing, and finally by the grace of God they rolled back. The Germans fell back. However, they would not quit and came back at us a second time, hard, very hard. They overran our position, knocking out our gun emplacements. Believe it or not, another fellow and I turned it around with a couple of their machine guns. Their regular gunners were killed. We jumped in and began firing. I don't know how many Germans we killed but it was one hell of a lot of them, many of them point blank right in front of the machine guns. I was so intent on killing them that I didn't give it a second thought. No. . . ."

Mr. Sloan sighed. "That's how I got the Silver Star. For gallantry in action, that's how the certificate reads. That's exactly what it says: 'gallantry in action.' I wear it every day, as you can see. I'm mighty proud of it. You can see it right here on my chest."

Mr. Sloan paused and it was clear that he was in deep thought and that emotions were overwhelming him. He undoubtedly was rethinking the battle. He had relived it with us. Now he was reliving it privately and could not bring himself back to the current situation. Tears rolled down his cheeks and he shook his head. Finally his eyes, which had glazed over, cleared and Mr. Sloan was with us again. He shook his head repeatedly and summarized, "It was one hell of a battle, one hell of a situation."

He wiped his eyes and nose, and drove on. But tears appeared again as he murmured, "And there were a lot of dead men. Yes, dead."

Wes and I remained silent out of respect for Mr. Sloan.

We rode along the scenic highway, impressed by the limestone cliffs that rose on both sides of the car. Wes and I looked at them closely and avoided any eye contact with Mr. Sloan. There were several places to pull the car over for especially scenic views but Mr. Sloan drove on in a determined way. We knew his driving was influenced by his memories. The memories of the battle, the fear and guilt, were never fully put to rest, but continued to haunt him.

As we approached Belle Fourche, Mr. Sloan regained his earlier composure and described Belle Fourche. "I've been stopping here for years as part of my tobacco route. Got some good customers here and they are friends too. If it's sightseeing you're after you won't find much here, excepting the beautiful countryside. Nothing of the Mt. Rushmore type."

"That's okay," I answered.

"'Course, newcomers like yourselves may turn something up. I will say it's the geographical center of the U.S. That doesn't give you anything to see, not even an official marker. That is still coming. The politicians have promised that."

"Anything else?" I asked.

"It was the home, if you can call it that, for Butch Cassidy and the Sundance Kid, at least for a while. People can't ever forget that. They talk about those two as if they were here yesterday."

I nodded and he continued. "You may not care to know that Belle Fourche is the center of the largest concentration of sheep in the whole U.S. And it brags about being the largest cattle shipping point in the world too. There may be things I haven't mentioned. Didn't think you would be interested. There's nothing really to see."

He drew a deep breath. "Boys, we've come to the end of our journey. I sure enjoyed talking to you. I'll drop you off at the next service station." He pulled into a station a short way ahead and ordered, "Fill 'er up. Get the windshield and check the oil."

Wes and I got out of the car, stood by the driver's door and talked for a few minutes longer. Mr. Sloan paid his bill and pulled out. Wes and I stood still for a few minutes trying to digest Mr. Sloan's war experience, especially all the feelings of it. After recovering a bit, we went into the service station to consider the facts that Mr. Sloan had given us about Belle Fourche. We agreed that having been the home of Butch Cassidy and the Sundance Kid, being the center of the U.S. and having more sheep than any other place in the country didn't give us anything to look at.

The service station attendant told us about two additional things. One was that there was a great rodeo held each year in the early days of July, but that was long over, so we dismissed it. The other was there was a small museum in town. Regrettably, its exhibits featured a unique doll collection. That was outside our interests. After exhausting the sightseeing possibilities Wes asked, "Is there a local park in which we might camp for a night?"

"Sure," the attendant answered. "Centennial Park. It's set up to keep the memory of the Old West alive, especially the cowboys. You'll see a statue up there of a cowboy riding high on a bucking bronco. It's not a camping park but you might find some place there to put up a tent. Anyway, try it. It doesn't look like you have a very big tent there. It might fit in." The attendant paused. "Maybe you should check out the right to camp there. Somebody at the museum can tell you. Check it, just to make sure. By the way, there's more to the museum than dolls. It will be worth your while to see it."

I looked at Wes for approval. He nodded his head and we left for the museum after getting the station attendant to hold our luggage for us.

The museum was much better than we expected and, as the attendant had suggested, had a more complete collection than dolls, particularly on the history of the Old West and Belle Fourche. Before leaving the museum we asked a studious looking woman in charge whether camping was permitted in

Centennial Park. She pleasantly told us it was okay and that it had exceptionally good facilities. We thanked her and were on our way.

"I liked the pioneer stuff, really liked it," Wes evaluated as we left the museum. "The doll stuff was pretty. That's not my thing, but I appreciated it."

We walked to the service station, picked up our luggage and found Centennial Park. "This is really a beauty," Wes said as we looked over the area. "And there are toilets and showers here."

"How about the statue of the cowboy riding a very wild horse, bucking?"

"God, it takes guts to do that. Not only are you likely to get bucked off, but you could be run over afterwards. There's nothing meaner than a wild horse."

After paying our respects to the cowboy we put up our tent. We shook the wrinkles out of it, looked over the scars left by the burning soot and agreed it would withstand any rain that might come. "This is great," I suggested. "It's close to the showers and toilets and there's a handy fire pot and a picnic table."

We stood looking at the tent for a few minutes when Wes complained, "I'm getting damned tired of those beans and the other canned stuff. Let's go to town—it's only about six blocks away—and buy ourselves a couple of steaks. We'll build up a great fire, let it burn down to coals and roast the steaks."

"That would really be a relief from the beans and spaghetti. Our budget can stand it. Shouldn't be more than fifty cents apiece. Maybe not even that much."

The butcher gave us more than a perfunctory glance as we entered his shop. He was baffled by our order of two thick steaks for roasting. "You boys new around here?" he inquired. "Don't believe I've seen you in here before."

"Just passing through, camping out. Having a special meal tonight," I answered.

"I can fix you up with just the right steak for dinner." He then turned and carefully cut a couple of sizeable pieces of meat off a side of beef. We were impressed but wondered what it would cost, probably more than we should be spending. He wrapped the steaks in special butcher's paper, a pink type of parchment, and announced, "That will be twenty-five cents apiece. Fifty cents total."

We were amazed. He smiled at our appreciation, and we left with a "thank you" and walked back to our campsite. After we walked away I asked, "Wes, do you think that butcher gave us a good price because he felt like we couldn't afford more?"

Wes was slow in responding. "I think you're right. He sized us up, how we looked, and thought we were in bad shape for money."

"It sure was nice of him to do that," I said and Wes nodded his head.

When we got back to the park we sat around a while, then took a shower, but given our limited clothes, had to put the same ones back on. We pulled a couple of small branches from a tree that overhung our tent and, using my jackknife, made two roasting sticks. We built a big fire that burned down to a good bed of coals. We attached our steaks to the roasting sticks, which were green and would not easily catch on fire. We turned our steaks over and over, being careful of our hands.

"Remember when we camped down on the James River and Reid was with us?" I asked. "It would be good to have him with us now."

Wes was quick to answer. "Sure, but it wouldn't be practical to have three people trying to hitchhike. Besides, his folks are so strict I don't think our lying about the trip would have worked. They would have figured out our plan sooner or later."

The steaks were roasted in about twenty minutes. The fat on the meat had dripped into the fire, causing large flames to jump up. They were great to watch and we continued to be careful of our hands and the roasting sticks as well. We could not afford to have one burn off and have the steak fall into the coals. We pulled the steaks from above the coals when we thought they were just the right color of brown and laid them on two pieces of bread. We ate them in the fashion of an open-face sandwich and with relish beyond anything we had experienced on the trip, excepting our hearty breakfast with Mr. Evans.

After eating the last morsel we turned to the peaches and followed the usual pattern of passing the can back and forth between us, making one spoon do for both of us. We sat around the campfire for a while afterward.

"It's great to be doing some real camping," I commented.

Wes followed, "God, yes. Especially since we've drug that damned tent all over the hell with us. First time we are really putting it to use."

"Not quite," I corrected. "Like we talked earlier, it helped us with the soot and the burning sparks on the freight outside Mitchell. And the rain and snake in the sand car. It's been a great tent."

"You're right. You're right," Wes agreed.

"And I am glad we pinned those blankets on the inside of the shelter halves. Otherwise we would be sleeping on the ground with only our clothes to keep us warm. I unpinned them and threw them on the ground. I don't know if you noticed, but I picked up a bunch of old newspapers at the service station and we'll put those underneath the blanket. That will keep the dampness away from us."

"I think we're ready to try it out," Wes said with enthusiasm. "You know, we don't have any pajamas, no front on the tent and only two blankets, one for the bottom and one of the top. But I'm ready for bed. It gets cold up here, and it's almost September. I hope all goes well tonight."

"I'm keeping all my clothes on and adding my jacket. If what we've heard is true, we'll need all of that."

We applied more of Mr. Jackson's lotion on our blisters, which were responding to the treatment. With that we climbed under the top blanket and were lulled to sleep by a hypnotic breeze that blew on the west side of the tent. I snuggled under the single blanket and passed from consciousness, but awoke several times during the night, each time with a chill. I tried desperately to crawl deeper into the blankets and escape the cold. Perhaps my imagination of greater warmth encouraged me back to sleep.

Morning finally came, introduced by bright sunlight that pressed some warmth into the doorway of the tent.

Chapter Six
Day Five: Campbell's Soup, Casino, Shy Anne's Rooms

"God, how we could have used a tent flap last night," Wes groaned. "We should have made one, however poor, before we left home."

I laughed. "Next time we'll do it."

I jumped out of the blankets, put on my shoes and left the tent to start a fire. There was plenty of wood around, along with waste paper in a garbage can. I soon had a blazing fire. We stood around the fire stiff from the cold. Finishing the last of our bread and a can of spaghetti, and with no verbal communication, we pulled the tent down, unbuttoned the two halves and laid them on the picnic table along with our suitcase. We pinned the blankets back on the shelter halves.

"We should get on the road early. Maybe a trucker or farmer will pick us up," I suggested.

"You don't mean a chicken farmer, do you?" Wes asked in order to bring some humor into our situation.

"Hell, no!" I answered, and with that we trudged to Highway 85.

"We ought to see Sturgis while we're up here. Deadwood, Silverton and Lead too," I said. "But Sturgis is the first town in line. The trip to Sturgis is only thirty or forty miles."

The walk warmed us, and when we stopped at the side of the highway we felt good about having seen Spearfish and Belle Fourche. I noted, "Great sightseeing and generous help from Tex Webster and his son Todd, and from Mr. Sloan. I'll never forget the generous butcher, whose name we'll never know."

We waited quite a while. Only a few cars passed us. In about forty-five minutes a neatly dressed man driving a new model Chevrolet stopped, looked us over carefully and asked, "What are your names? Where are you going, and why?"

We responded quickly as he continued to scrutinize us.

"I'm Bill Yates and I've been traveling this territory for fourteen years. I know it like the back of my hand—every place and everybody. So, you're Carl and you're Wes?" he noted, pointing at us. "Couldn't have two finer names. No sir, couldn't have two finer names.

"Get in front with me. It will be crowded but there's no room in back. Got nothing but cans of soup back there. Campbell's Soup, that's what I sell and I'm proud of it."

He waxed about it all the way to Sturgis. He ended up by saying, "I'll be here about two hours. Got to call on several stores, then I'm on to Deadwood, Lead and Silverton." He thought a moment. "I'll tell you what. Meet me here at noon and we'll get some hamburgers and be on our way to Deadwood. If you like, I'll drop you off there. In the meantime, you can look around Sturgis."

He parked his Chevrolet in front of a grocery store. Wes and I got out at the same time as Mr. Yates and started taking our luggage with us, feeling we couldn't leave it entrusted to a man who was going to make a number of stops in town. Then too, Bill Yates talked so much and easily, we didn't know whether we could trust him. He seemed a little light to us, one whose talk probably was more than his doing.

But he interrupted us. "Don't bother lugging that stuff around with you. You may want to do some fast sightseeing. The stuff will be okay in the car."

We reluctantly left the luggage and walked onto the sidewalk as Bill Yates disappeared into the store.

It took us about twenty minutes to walk up and down Main Street. "There's nothing going on here now," Wes said. "But judging from the number of bars, the nightlife must be pretty good. Things must really jump."

"Yeah, I saw pictures of dancing girls who put on nightly shows. You know, at least at two bars. Maybe more."

"In spite of our best planning," Wes said with a sly look on his face, "we didn't work any nightlife into our tour."

"That's right," I agreed. "We've had nothing but pure sightseeing since we've been traveling."

"Well," Wes concluded, "we're not going to be here tonight, so we have to give up the idea of nightlife."

We moved away from the bars and drifted into the city park and read a plaque about the town's stormy past:

IN ITS GLORIOUS PAST STURGIS HAD CATTLEMEN AND SHEEPMEN FIGHTING EACH OTHER, AND BOTH FIGHTING THE RUSTLERS, GAMBLERS, CARD SHARKS AND GUNMEN. YET ALL FOUND HOMES IN STURGIS. SOME PROSPERED, SOME WERE KILLED AND OTHERS MOVED ON. MARSHALS, SOMETIMES ONE STEP AHEAD OF THE LAW THEMSELVES, KILLED AND WERE KILLED.

This wild history was so different from the peaceful, mundane history of Sioux Center, where thrifty, straight-laced, hardworking farmers set the tone of the area. Gunfights, gambling, prostitution and range wars were not part of its background. There were early wars with the Sioux as the whites pushed them off their lands, but the Army took care of the fighting and left the settling of the land in the hands of the whites.

We read another plaque about Fort Meade, which was very near Sturgis, and we noted its having provided a home for the U.S. Cavalry back in the days when such was important. As we walked back to the store where Mr. Yates left us we talked about what we had just seen, trying to absorb it. When we reached the spot where the car had been parked, we noticed it was gone.

"Geez, I hope he didn't leave without us," Wes cried out.

"Remember, he said he had to call on several grocery stores. I guess he must be on that route. Let's check the street. It won't take long."

We started down one side of the street and then walked up the other, looking for Mr. Yates' Chevrolet. Our anxiety mounted as we searched and searched for Mr. Yates' car without success. There was a break in our worry as we encountered another plaque. This one, however, was not in bronze but a sign that was framed and attached to one of the older buildings. It read:

"Some real fun must have gone on there," Wes laughed and I joined him. Our fun was short-lived as we realized Bill Yates' car was not to be discovered. We walked back to the store where we had left him and took a position and waited. It was twelve forty-five now and there was still no sign of Mr. Yates.

Wes turned to me. "You know, it doesn't make any difference about how nice people are, and Mr. Yates is one of those, but when it gets right down to it, you can't trust them. Here we are hanging around and hanging around and the guy doesn't show up. And our luggage is gone."

"Don't be too hard on him. Maybe he's having a hard time, really hard time, making a sale. We just don't know anything about the business he's in."

"Well, it shouldn't take much time to find out if a store owner wants a case of Campbell's Soup. Either the store owners want it or don't want it. That's how it seems to me."

"That's only partly true. Maybe he's pushing some kind of a deal. Like, if you buy a case or two of Campbell's Soup, a case of pork and beans will only be seventy percent of the usual price. You know, that kind of thing. Or the store owner may not be paying his bills and Mr. Yates is trying to get him to pay up and make a sale at the same time. Or maybe he's good friends with some of the store people and they are having a good visit. You never know."

Wes threw his hands up in the air. "I still say he should have let us know. Right now it looks like we are stranded and without our tent and suitcase filled with food! And what's more, we don't know what to do."

I suggested, "Let's ask this store owner what he knows of Mr. Yates' schedule."

We went into the store and encountered a very tall, round-shouldered man, probably in his early sixties. He had on a soiled brown apron and visor on his head in the fashion of a newspaper editor. His face was gentle and its lines fit in with his easy smile. He looked like the owner. I cautiously asked, "Do you know where Mr. Yates went after leaving here?"

"Boys, you're asking about the toughest question you could ask. Who knows? He was in here sure enough, but that was a while ago, maybe an hour. But I don't know whether he went to call on Zinder or Sheldon, both my competitors. Now Zinder is just down the street about a block. The Sheldons are up a little ways the opposite direction, about two or three blocks. You should check there. Boys, I wish you luck, because I know he's a hard guy to keep up with." Belatedly he asked, "Do you know I'm Mr. Wirth?"

We nodded and left.

After that we called on Zinder. He was a hefty, two hundred and fifty pounder. He had the attitude of an angry football coach, simply saying, "He was here but left a while ago. Nothing against him personally, but glad to see him go. Can be a pest!"

We didn't like to hear criticism of a person as kind as Mr. Yates but took it in stride and left to check Sheldon's.

A motherly person, Mrs. Sheldon was an in-charge type. She was friendly and, like Mr. Wirth, wore an apron. Hers, however, was clean and not spotted. She greeted us like boys having all the characteristics of being lost. She was no real help. "Left here about fifteen or twenty minutes ago. I have no idea where he went."

"Well, I'm afraid he left us. It's one-thirty now, over an hour after he said he'd pick us up. I sure hate to lose our luggage and the tent but I don't know what we can do about it. I felt we should have taken our luggage with us, but he was so sure we should leave it, that it would be okay."

While I lamented, Wes suggested, "Let's go to the edge of town and hitch it back to Rapid City. We need a place to sleep tonight. We'll skip Lead and Deadwood. I've given up on Mr. Yates."

I nodded in dismay. "He sure left us in a bad situation."

We walked to the edge of town, grumbling and damning Mr. Yates when we heard the blast of a car horn. We turned and our depression jumped to elation, more to recover our luggage than to see Mr. Yates.

He called to us as he stopped the car. "I guess you boys gave up on me. It took me longer to strike a deal with this one fellow who kept saying I was giving his competition up the street a better deal, and he took some convincing that I wasn't. He knew I wasn't but he kept trying to get me to lower my price for him. I felt like swatting him, giving him one hell of a blow, but, of course, I couldn't do that. So I had to humor him. To beat all, he took me over the Beavers' Club after the sale for a drink. If you couldn't find me, it was because I drove him over there. That's several blocks off the main drag."

"You make the sale?" Wes inquired.

"Yes, and I didn't lower my price." Mr. Yates, changing his tone, said, "Now, boys, I think I said something about hamburgers earlier. So I better make good on that, especially after leaving you stranded, or at least you thought you were."

He drove back to Sturgis, stopping in front of a cafe, Rosy's. "Rosy handles the cooking herself, and while I never have eaten a full meal here, she does real well on hamburgers."

This turned out to be true, as she served not only a good hamburger but a great side dish of french fries.

"You boys look awfully hungry," Mr. Yates observed, and shouted, "Rosy, these boys each need another hamburger, and make them your best!"

Wes and I shook our heads in consternation and approval, and exclaimed at the same time, "Thank you."

"I owe it to you for standing you up. You must have wondered where in tarnation I was."

We shrugged our shoulders in a neutral way and I suggested, "Forget it. We figured you'd pick us up if we didn't get a ride first, and that's just what happened."

We left the cafe and as Mr. Yates got the car back on the highway he picked up a different vein. "Boys, I don't know what you are thinking of for a job, or profession, but you ought to think about business. That's where the challenge is. That's where the money is. I'm in the sales end. My job is a little one, but it's a good one. I'm satisfied."

Mr. Yates only stopped to catch his breath. "You fellows are young, so you ought to figure on something bigger. Start wherever you can, grab an opportunity, whether it's a hamburger joint like Rosy's or something bigger, like industrial sales, for example, selling heavy machinery. But get started, keep your eyes open and work your way up. Whether it's making something or selling it, go for making a profit, earning a commission, getting ahead."

Mr. Yates left no topic untouched. "And don't forget today's world. You got to get trained first, trained in business—accounting, purchasing, marketing, business management and employee supervision—all of these things and more."

Mr. Yates' plans for us seemed ready to escalate to Harvard, General Motors and beyond. But Wes's question brought him back to the reasonable. "Take Rosy's place. Not much to it, at least not so it looks to the outsider, but you have to have a building, you have to buy it or rent it, and if you own it you have to maintain it. Then you've got to have employees—a cook, maybe two, and waitresses. There is purchasing to take care of—hamburger, potatoes, peanut oil for fixing the french fries, salt and pepper, catsup and stuff for the salads, plus beverages. In the meantime you'd be busy lobbying to get the politicians to issue you a license to sell beer."

Before Wes could continue Mr. Yates broke in. "You've got the right idea. You'd have to handle the whole system and get customers to come in, and come again and again to buy what you're selling, and you've got to have your prices right to make a profit and to keep people returning, so the prices have to be just right."

We began to wonder whether Mr. Yates and his reluctant customer hadn't finished their negotiations with a tip or two too many out of the bottle.

Mr. Yates slowed down. "We probably have pushed the hamburger business too far. I'll stop but will add, consider business, boys. Consider business."

I chuckled to myself, thinking, This is so complicated to me that I'll surely have to see about getting into the Harvard Business School.

"Lead is just around the next corner and then Deadwood. Sometimes they are called the twin cities. You look them all over." He laughed and then continued, "I don't want you trying to steal any gold from the Homestake Gold Mine, even though it is the richest in the world. The other thing is, I don't want you getting any bad ideas when you're up in the cemetery looking at the graves of Wild Bill Hickock and Calamity Jane. They've only got bad lessons to teach."

Mr. Yates' talk was interrupted by the occasional traffic of Deadwood. He wove through it and stopped at a gas station. "Boys, this is Deadwood. I'll drop you right here. This is close to the cemetery. I don't want to depress you, but you might want to visit it."

Mr. Yates stopped and with a salute said, "Best of luck to you and don't forget what I told you. Go into business!"

Wes and I looked at each other with a sense of relief. We pulled our luggage from the car. Though worn, we were so pleased to have it. After we thanked Mr. Yates for the ride and lunch, he drove away and Wes exclaimed, "I've never been so glad to have anything in my whole life as this beat-up luggage. I don't know what he was thinking of back there in Sturgis but it surely wasn't us. We might have lost this luggage, which was our food and shelter. Besides, how would we ever be able to pay Clarence for the tent?"

I was more moderate. "He was making a deal, making his living, and to the extent that he gave us a thought, he may have figured we could wait. Then, on the other hand, he may have been so deep into the deal he lost track of time."

"Don't forget the drinks he was having over at the Beavers Club!"

"I guess you're right. One additional thing about Mr. Yates: he's really carried away with business. He sure enough wants us to get into it, especially the hamburger business!"

We began to laugh and for several minutes could not stop. I kidded, "I can just see you flipping hamburgers, making salads, frying french fries and smiling at the girls."

My joshing encouraged Wes to respond in kind. "And I can just see you doing the same with one of those military-like skull caps on, mopping up the counter and pushing bad hamburgers onto customers. And as I think about it I can just see the advertisement on your cap, WES AND CARL'S FOR THE BEST!

After our laugh we gave up Mr. Yates. Wes helped make the shift. "From what I've read, Deadwood was a brawling mining town. That means there was a lot of reckless hell-raising going on, maybe some that has carried over. We ought to find out. So let's wait with the cemetery and graves of these hard-core cases until later. First let's take in Main Street. There must have been a lot of action right there and I hope there's some left."

I agreed but differed somewhat. "I think the action will really take place at night, not during the day. Though maybe there's a little action around gambling. I read that gambling is a big thing here in Deadwood. Saw it in some of the folders that Mr. Evans gave us. So let's have a look at it."

We convinced the attendant at the service station to store our luggage to give us greater freedom. "Okay, it'll be right here but don't leave it longer than today. We can't be responsible."

We agreed and started down the street, picking up the spirit of recklessness that gambling suggested. We went into a couple of casinos. I hid my shyness with a bold exterior which would not have fooled anybody, were they to have been interested. Wes, on the other hand, didn't need to hide a shyness because he didn't have it. Instead, he walked around confidently, looking at the various activities. We were surprised at the number of serious gamblers at the card tables and the scattering of persons, including old ladies, pulling the arms of the slot machines.

After we left the second casino we stopped on the sidewalk. "My God, those people are reckless with their money," Wes pointed out. "The chance of their winning is stacked against them. Doesn't make any difference whether it's the slot machines, which are fixed in favor of the house, or whether it's a card game at the gaming table. The favor is always for the house!"

"So why do they keep playing?" I asked.

Wes shrugged. "I don't know. Remember, Mr. Hanson talked about that kind of thing. He didn't understand it either but said something about 'hope springs eternal.' "

We didn't settle the question, but left it and walked down the street. I sensed Wes's confidence was high and mine had risen after having been in two casinos without having been hurt. At that point we saw a striking building, not for its stately architecture, but for its gaudiness. Painted a bright red, it had many flashing lights of different colors framing the door. As if drawn by a magnet we approached it and immediately saw its double doors were wide open. We peered in and saw its inside decoration got its cue from the outdoor decor, that is, it had a lot of tinsel and bright lights hung low over the gaming tables, which were covered with deep green, rich looking felt. The lights were framed in shades of different colored glass, and strips of silver and gold aluminum streamers, like some I had seen over used car lots, crisscrossed the room. They waved back and forth, blown by an invisible fan. Spirited music, jazz, filled the room. It was pitched at just the right level—not too loud or too soft.

I could see, even in the brief look into the room, that the most serious gamblers were served drinks—and not just Coca Colas—and sandwiches right at their tables while gambling. Many things were happening so fast I didn't have a chance to think them all over, but I did decide that such service had not been given to Wes and me when we were earning money for this trip cleaning basements, washing windows and that kind of thing. No, we never had anybody treat us that well. I reasoned there was something special here besides the drinks and sandwiches.

A bold sign resting on the sidewalk announced:

LIMITED GAMBLING WAGERS: NO MINIMUM, MAXIMUM OF
$5
DRESS CODE: COME AS YOU ARE
DEALERS ARE FRIENDLY, WON'T HURRY YOU

We moved back to look in the wide open double doors and oversized room. We heard yelling and music in the background.

"The cemetery will have to wait," Wes concluded. "This was just made for us."

In addition to the blinking lights and fast music, several scantily dressed cocktail hostesses paraded around inside. I liked what I saw but was intimidated. However, an underlying impulse to get into the scene provoked my head to nod. I was ready to join in some way or another, yet I was mindful of the condition of our clothes, especially after having slept in them in Belle Fourche. But the sign had said COME AS YOU ARE, and I believed it and I sensed Wes did too, or he didn't care.

A hostess saw us at the doorway with a look of great anticipation. She stepped out, and with a comely smile encouraged, "You're most welcome to come in and look around. We need some younger fellows."

Wes returned her smile and I gulped, especially as I checked over the shortness of her dress and her beautiful legs. As my eyes moved upward they caught the lowness of her blouse or whatever she was wearing. I knew it wasn't called a blouse. It didn't have enough material to be called a blouse!

Wes had great presence. "Haven't I seen you in Rapid City? You look exactly like Betty that I met there."

The girl was experienced, to be sure, with such simple get-acquainted techniques and answered, "How strange. I'm from Rapid, but I've been up here at the Flash Casino for seven months."

Wes was not to be outmaneuvered. "I would have sworn, but you may be right. I'm sure you are. But it's great to meet you now. I'm sorry I hadn't met you in the past."

I stood in the background as Wes entered the doorway. He continued, "Could it be that you're Patsy?"

"What makes you say that?" the waitress asked, and being attracted by Wes's attention she repeated, "What makes you say that?" She smiled broadly and gave a subtle shiver to her shoulders.

Wes's facial blisters had healed, and the shiny red skin that remained gave him a peculiar, distinguished look. It seemed that the comely hostess was attracted by it. She scanned his face again and again and offered him an encouraging smile.

Wes responded, "Patsy sounds just right for you. So right because you have such a pretty smile and all." He emphasized the "all."

I wondered where this might be going when the hostess said straight out, "My name is Martha. Don't like it. So I go by the name of Dot."

"Where did you get that?" Wes pursued.

"Well, if you have to know, the bartender gave it to me."

"I wonder, do you think I could get a job tending bar here?"

"Oh, you!" Dot responded, obviously enjoying the attention.

He continued his advance. "Is he your special?"

"I can't say," Dot answered demurely. "Maybe and maybe not."

Wes pressed on. "How heavy do you lean on the 'not' side? You have to know that's the side I'm on. That's right, that's the side I'm on, and waiting."

Dot's eyes tightened just a bit and then became intense. Wes seemed to have reached her with that. After a pause she said, "Are you serious?"

Wes kept going. "You'll have to try me to know."

Dot pulled back just a bit and whispered a nearly imperceptible "No."

I figured Wes was threatening for Dot, though her dress suggested that such talk as Wes's was a fitting proposition. But the dress was misleading. It was the uniform of the day for the casino and may have had little relationship to the person wearing it.

After Wes made his last remark, Dot offered, "I'm not sure, but maybe under different circumstances than here at the casino we could carry this farther, but we're limited as to what we can do here."

Wes had made such headway I wondered whether another similarly clad waitress might visit with me, give me a chance to get acquainted. My thought was interrupted as Dot suggested with an attractive smile, "Why don't you boys come in and look around. We're delighted to have you. We really are." She included me in her welcome so I moved forward, but Wes stepped right alongside of Dot. I was surprised he didn't take her

106

arm, just to test out his progress. I also wondered about the bartender, the genius who had named her Dot. Might he take Wes in hand? I pushed that disturbing thought from my mind and stepped to the other side of Dot. I knew she was responding to Wes so I scanned the gaming room looking for a second hostess, one as comely as Dot. We had been on this Black Hills trip for several days, though it seemed much longer, and I clearly needed some feminine attention. Benevolent drivers, beans, spaghetti, peaches and a pup tent weren't enough.

Though I was looking hard, using all the powers my eyes could muster, I didn't have to try that hard, as a young, especially attractive woman was immediately to my left and away from Dot and Wes. Having observed the success of Wes's approach gave me confidence. I walked over to her and said the same thing Wes had said to Dot. "Haven't I seen you before? Maybe Rapid City?" After that I bent the truth and ventured, "That's where I'm from." Hoping to pick up some prestige for myself, I followed with, "That's quite a city." I tried a broad and, hopefully, engaging smile.

The beautiful young thing, not any older than I, or so I imagined, put me down. "Now sonny, aren't you pushing it a bit?"

In all the sincerity I could gather I gasped, "Oh, no. I am really trying to meet you," and added with a hopeful note, "I really am."

"Some other time." And with that the beautiful young thing walked out of my life. My heart hit the floor, especially as she approached another patron, who I figured was a prospect for the gaming table.

Wes continued his success. He now was walking arm in arm with Dot toward a gaming table, and I said to myself with anxiety, "He doesn't know a damned thing about poker. Nothing. What is he getting into?" And for the moment I gave up looking for another hostess.

Dot's grasp of Wes's arm meant business, gambling business. I was so worried about him I missed the large, uniformed house detective walking toward us. Wes was up front, nearing the gaming table. The detective got to him first. He was polite but very certain about what he was doing. He dismissed Dot. "I think the management wants you back at the office." He then turned to Wes and gently said, "Son, unless you have identification that you are eighteen, you can't be in here. It's out of bounds for juveniles."

Wes was shaken to lose Dot, who disappeared ever so quickly. More basically, he was shaken by being called a juvenile and kicked out, though politely, from this flashy gambling joint. "But you allow older ladies in here," Wes pointed out, implying that even though he was only a teenager he was every bit as responsible as the elderly women.

"What's that got to do with you?"

Wes tried to explain, but was unsuccessful and the detective followed with, "Sorry," and put his hand gently on his shoulder.

Wes had a great sense of humor and was not about to let this experience in the casino go sour. "Officer, it is good of you to tell us. Be sure we meant no harm."

The officer ate it up and commented gently, "So I'll just ask you to step outside."

Wes nodded, but not before telling the officer, "Be sure to tell Dot I'm looking forward to seeing more of her!"

Though perplexed, the officer led us to the door.

"It was great while it lasted," Wes laughed. "Just didn't last long enough."

"Wes, I have to give it to you. The way you and Dot were moving ahead, all you needed was some privacy." I changed my tone and said, "It's a hell of a time to suggest the cemetery, but let's go up there to see the graves. I don't care to do it, but since we're here I guess we should."

"It was damned unfair getting kicked out of there," Wes said, expressing his disappointment. "I was just beginning to make some headway. Just beginning. But since there are more than twenty such places here, I might just try it again."

"You were lucky. Lucky that baby, Dot, didn't get you into a game of blackjack, poker or whatever they were playing."

"No way. I was just enjoying my walk with her, and if we had gotten to the card table I would have put my arm on her shoulder ever so easily and said, 'I just want to watch and see how this goes.' "

"Then what?"

"I would have played it by ear and enjoyed the moment. What more can you ask? You have to work with what is given."

I shook my head in amazement. "I don't know how you do it, to get the girls to follow you right along. I watched and tried exactly the same thing with another one of those cuties with the short shorts and less of a top, and I didn't get any place. I couldn't even get the girl to give me a second look. I didn't quite get what she said but it was something like 'Bug off!' "

"I wouldn't put any stock into my getting next to Dot or into what happened. It was just that Dot had the house assignment to get people to the gaming tables, and even though I was a poor prospect she went through her duties. That was okay with me. I was enjoying it and had my eyes open."

I shook my head. Though Wes had given me more of an idea about what he was doing, I was still amazed and gave my last word on him and Dot. "That's all true, but I saw more than a twinkle in her eye during that carrying on."

Wes did not answer, but turned to another thing. "Let's get out to see the graves of some real characters. It's not far to the Mt. Moriah Cemetery."

As we entered the grounds I found the grave of Wild Bill Hickock and remarked, "I see that Wild Bill Hickock had twenty-one notches on his gun, had been a Civil War scout, a stagecoach guard, hunting guide and town marshal. All jobs took speed and deadly aim with firearms. He came right here to Deadwood in June of 1876 and was killed two months later. Must have been a very, very tough place."

Wes chimed in, "If there ever was a wild west character it was Calamity Jane. Her grave is right over here. She was a hard-living woman who looked, dressed, drank, cussed and shot like a man. Her stone says she drove a bull train from Cheyenne to Deadwood around 1876. Though known for her toughness, she nursed many children with diphtheria during an epidemic they had here."

I called back, "Here's another real character to know about. It's Poker Alice. Her grave is over here. She was a businesswoman over at Sturgis but she is buried here. She ran a gambling house and brothel to entertain the servicemen from Fort Meade. She liked her whiskey smooth and her cigars big!"

We came out of the cemetery and realized that much of the afternoon had passed. We walked back toward the casino area and Wes asked, "Where did we see the great sign, SHY ANNE'S ROOMS? We might want to spend the night there."

"We can't afford it. No way. We've only got about twelve or thirteen dollars left."

"That's a lot . . . a lot," Wes argued. "I found being in the tent awfully cold. So if we can spend a night in a rooming house and do it for very little money, I'm all for the rooming house. Now where did you see that sign? And do you remember what it was called?"

"It's called Shy Anne's Rooms. It looked like it was on the second floor of a saloon. It's just back about a block. Funny thing is, the sign was trimmed in lace like you see sewed to the bottoms of women's petticoats. Another funny thing, the sign didn't say Cheyenne Rooms or having any bucking horses to set it off. No, it just said Shy Anne's Rooms and had the lace around it. What do you make of that?"

"I figure it might be a place where you can make out, you know, sexually!" Wes answered, and casually suggested, "On the other hand, it might be a real genuine rooming house, just a plain rooming house. We should look it over." He rubbed his head. "Just in case it's a real rooming house we ought to have our suitcase. We'll need a change of clothes tomorrow. Besides, if it's a rooming house we have to make the right appearance when we go in to look it over. A suitcase would make us look real."

I continued to protest but Wes stayed on his track. "We'll walk back to the service station, pick up our suitcase, get the attendant to keep the pup tent until tomorrow, come back and check out Shy Anne's Rooms."

Wes was a strong person and though I felt we might be walking into a disaster I went along with him. Without any further words being spoken we returned to the service station, got our suitcase and talked the attendant into keeping our shelter halves for another day.

Walking more quickly than usual we returned to the sign that had caused all the curiosity. We looked up at it and noted especially the frilly lace around the print. Then we saw a stairway that led up to Shy Anne's place.

Shifting from foot to foot I asked Wes, "What will we say when we get up there?"

"Depends on how we see it. We will start with finding out whether she rents rooms, if that's for real. Or if she only rents out beds with girls in them." He was determined and had both feet firmly planted on the sidewalk. That Wes was taking the lead in this search for information, and probably fun, was clear. "Let's just see if we can find Shy Anne. Bring the suitcase and let's go."

My hesitancy evaporated. I gripped the handle of the suitcase and followed him up the dimly lit stairway. The steps had some cakes of dirt on them, as if some uncleaned heels had traveled these stairs after a recent rain. I figured that whether it was a rooming house or something more exciting, the stairs should have been scrubbed, and painted for good measure. Some real clods must have climbed these stairs.

Wes reached the top of the stairs as I was still thinking about their condition. He boldly inspected the entryway but didn't have much to look at. A light bulb hung on a cord from the ceiling and brightened the doorway, but only so-so. The door stood out against the rest of the dingy hallway. It was cardinal red! The paint was enamel, very shiny.

"Hmmm," Wes mused as he looked the situation over and then pressed the doorbell. It was ringed by a circle of cut glass made to look like diamonds and formed in the shape of a heart. My blood pressure must have zoomed up, as my heart was hitting the insides of my rib cage with the heavy strokes of a sledgehammer.

After less than a minute we heard the latch give way and a small crack appeared between the frame and the door. I figured, "What a strange way to do business. If Shy Anne really wants to rent rooms she should open the door widely and welcome us. Or if she is occupied and doesn't have time to greet us, she should have posted a welcome sign." Yet Shy Anne didn't do either and my tension continued to rise.

Finally, in more time than I had hoped for, a whisper came through the crack, "Have you been here before?"

"No. No," Wes replied, and to assure her, "My friend and I are looking for a room for tonight."

There was a pause and finally the voice, though still tentative, took an unusual tone, one that mixed persuasion with rejection. "All night might be more than you want to spend. Most of our clients stay for much less time. Maybe an hour. A few stay for a couple of hours. But we do have an occasional client who stays all night, and if that's what you want we can arrange it. Yes. Please feel you are most welcome."

I wasn't sure how Wes understood the woman but he boldly replied, "You probably haven't seen our suitcase, it's being hidden behind the door, but we want an all night deal. We can't go back out wandering on the street after we've had a start here. We need a whole night's rest." He emphasized, "A whole night's rest."

I stood in the background and continued to hold the suitcase, though I was not aware of it. I was too involved in following the conversation, too inquisitive about the person behind the door and too afraid of what we were getting into. I continued to clutch the suitcase.

Wes facing the slit in the door, putting forth his most persuasive smile, and me standing behind him with the luggage, reminded me of our position on the highway when Wes had his thumb up and smiling for a ride. Or better yet, it reminded me of our casino experience where he had engaged Dot, the card table hostess. However, he was not thumbing a ride now but talking to either a dog-in- the-manger rooming house clerk or a madam of a bordello.

Wes tried hard to make face-to-face contact with this strange person, using just the right tone of voice. I admired his know-how and scolded myself for lacking such skill. "We are just a couple of young athletes traveling the Hills and needing a night's rest," he intoned. "Just a couple of young athletes." He emphasized "young."

That did it. The slit in the door slowly opened wider and we got a partial view of the secretive woman inside. And she got a glimpse of us. Finally she pulled the door all the way open. When I saw her and the manner in which she was dressed I thought I heard John Philip Sousa playing "Hail to the Chief." The trumpets and trombones blared and they were backed up by a strong baritone and bass section.

Shy Anne stood there—at least I thought it was she. Her eyes were blue and soft. She was thin, maybe too thin, and not much older than ourselves. Though tense, she appeared to be a kind woman who didn't belong in this business. I thought business because I had almost ruled out that this was a rooming house. Most amazing was her dress. It was in the fashion of the hostesses at the casino—a scanty panty and brassiere combination gilded by silver and gold sequins. This outfit covered only a small part of her body that it intended to cover and left most of her uncovered. Her stockings were sheer and I couldn't figure out where or how they were attached. I decided I had spent enough time trying to figure that out, when I could not see any way of succeeding.

I felt Shy Anne was conscious of my staring so I started to look directly into her eyes, hoping to make contact with some feeling, but I was distracted as I noticed she wore a pair of sequin-covered pumps—sequins of silver and gold like her panty and brassiere affair. They were in the elegant style of Judy Garland. With all of my looking I decided that Shy Anne was well proportioned, with an emphasis on her breasts. They seemed unusually large, but it may have been the fact that they were more uncovered than covered that made them look large.

Wes wasn't as carried away with Shy Anne. Instead, he concentrated on his approach. Mixing enthusiasm, casualness and courting, he gently asked, "Are you Shy Anne?"

That really did something for Shy Anne, or maybe she pretended that it did. She nodded, smiled with what looked like appreciation and in a low whisper answered, "Yes." Though it was only one word, it seemed to carry so much more with it. It

113

sent rockets off in my head and I got the feeling we were attending royalty. However, Shy Anne did not extend herself beyond that, and John Phillip Sousa's band continued playing "Hail to the Chief."

Wes followed with, "We saw your sign downstairs. It's quite clear that you have rooms so we came up to see what you offer."

This brought a slight smile to Shy Anne's face that carried amusement and a special suggestiveness. We were still standing, and uncomfortably so. I was still holding the suitcase and being unaware of it because I was entranced and bewildered by Shy Anne. The suitcase, which had an illustrative history in my family, was in danger of being lodged in a low-class rooming house or something worse.

I felt it was endangered because my dear mother had bought it several years before for a family train trip to visit relatives in North Dakota. Along with seeking a practical grip for her clothes, my mother wanted the suitcase to represent the position and means of the family. So she purchased it at an upscale leather shop on a shopping trip to Yankton. There was nothing like that in Sioux Center. The leather suitcase, called a Gladstone, was the best that money could buy. So it represented our hoped-for prestige as it stood on railroad platforms and in the houses of relatives. My mother was a modest woman; however, if just the right moment presented itself, she called attention to the "Gladstone." The trip was successful, though the Gladstone got a few scratches on it caused by reckless baggage handlers. My mother regretfully accepted the damage as the price to pay to having one's baggage checked and handled, and she continued to display it whenever possible.

Those scratches were the first of many that were inflicted on the Gladstone over the next five years. More trips, more scratches. The worst of them came when a relative, Aunt Lucy, knowing about the high quality Gladstone, borrowed it for a trip all the way to the west coast. When Aunt Lucy returned a scarred up Gladstone, my mother was annoyed but said nothing as Aunt Lucy gushed about the help the Gladstone was to her. "I just don't know what I would have done without it, and it made me so proud to show it off wherever I went."

My mother remained silent but frowned, put the Gladstone to rest on the floor and later put it into a closet.

That west coast trip broke the prestige-back of the Gladstone. It was just too scarred up now to be used for show. So I was free to use it on camping trips, including several with the Boy Scouts, where it was used as a kind of small coffee table in the middle of our tent.

Yet as I stood there holding the beaten-up Gladstone at Shy Anne's, I stood holding history and family tradition. So when I became conscious that I was still holding the suitcase I was less embarrassed than I would have been with a lesser suitcase, that is, with something less than a Gladstone.Aware of being in some kind of low class joint—whatever it might be—and not wanting to put the Gladstone down, I held onto it.

Shy Anne felt the awkwardness of the situation and, extended her hand to a brightly covered sofa, and suggested we sit down. The sofa was a mix of gaudy colors, but the major color was a bright red. I remembered one just like it in the second hand store in Sioux Center, and I wondered why she chose it for her reception room. As I was about to sit down, I again became aware that I was holding the Gladstone, awkwardly put it on the floor, sat down and settled back.

Continuting to extend her hand. Shy Anne glided to an overstuffed chair nearby. With my eyes glued on her I saw that the chair was covered with the same bright material as the sofa. Again the idea of the second hand store came to mind. I fought off the association and became captivated by Shy Anne's fingernails. They were highly polished with a purple colored film that matched her heavily spread lipstick. Long earrings fell from her ears. Delicate little chains held sets of brightly cut glass made to imitate jewels. They swayed back and forth whenever Shy Anne turned her head. I watched them sway back and forth and began to feel woozy and realized I had to attend to something else or go under.

Shy Anne's narrow, sensitive face, exceptionally white skin and bright eyes, set far apart, got my attention away from the swinging of her earrings. Her face was topped by blonde hair that seemed overly white, probably helped along with peroxide.

Shy Anne was all for style, and the dramatic upsweep of her hair to a knot at the top of her head made that clear. It was held in place with the help of two or three large white combs—white probably to match her hair. As I sat there drinking this all up, I fantasized how she would look if the combs were removed and her hair were allowed to drop down onto her shoulders. Surely she would have less of a Martha Washington look. I gave this idea up quickly as I got a companion idea—that is, of me embracing her and undoing her hair.

I was enamored by the idea but finally gave it up as I noticed a heavy gold chain around her neck which held an exceptionally large cross. I wondered if Shy Anne might be mixing religion into her work. But religion or not, she sure was all for decoration and I wondered what she would like at Christmas. Religion aside, the cross rested exactly where her ample bosom split. I watched and watched the cross until I realized it was having a hypnotic effect on me. Not knowing what else to do, I distracted myself by looking at the floor. I was trying hard to "cool it," though I felt I was being rude by my inattentiveness.

I didn't have to worry long, as Shy Anne subtly pulled my concentration back to her agenda. She gently pushed one of the combs firmly back into place and I caught the gentle sweep of her hand. Several bracelets dangled around her right wrist, and as I looked more closely I saw she had a comparative array on her left wrist. Adding to the display were the rings on her right hand—one for every finger! To Shy Anne's credit she did not make an obvious display of her jewelry—her decorations—but made them a distinct part of her whole person.

Though she was a strange being to my eyes, I imagined her as a member of our English class back in Sioux Center, without all of her jewelry, without her makeup, with her hair down from the top of her head and resting on her shoulders or cut short like other members of the class. Just sitting there like the rest of us, not trying to enchant anyone. I even wondered how she would attempt to capture the significance of Chaucer. That notion didn't last long, as I knew it was completely out of this world. Sioux Center's English class at the sophomore or junior level was not Shy Anne's thing. I did ponder when she had left school and why. She was so young she really belonged there.

I had all of these ideas flashing through my head as Wes and Shy Anne were looking back and forth at each other. Wes was going at it like I had seen Clark Gable do in the movies, at least that's what it looked like to me. And Shy Anne seemed to like it, as I saw her give him a couple of gentle half smiles and her eyes give him just a little twinkle, not a whole one but just a bit of one.

All of this had gone on, time had passed, but Shy Anne had never answered Wes's real question about coming upstairs to learn what Shy Anne had to offer. I didn't know, but I thought she'd just let Wes guess, make a game out of it. Wes, however, was not put off. "What does that lace around the sign outside mean, and the specially decorated doorbell? What are they for?"

Coyly Shy Anne answered quietly, "It has to do with the excitement we offer, the pleasure we give, the fun we generate."

As I admired her use of "generate" and speculated where she got it, and decided it was from radio commercials, Shy Anne raised her voice just a little until it took on a husky quality, though still gentle, and asked, "Doesn't lace and a heart make you think of exciting things?"

I was perplexed by the question for just a second or two because the first thing lace made me think of was women's petticoats and the curtains in our living room back home. Then my mind got after Shy Anne's question, after it in greater depth, and I was electrified by the idea of fun and excitement with Shy Anne. In my experience fun and excitement meant sports football, basketball, track. But I knew immediately that there weren't to be any sports here, at least not football or basketball! But some real excitement of a different kind!

"Hm," Wes kind of hummed, then asked a question that wasn't in tune with Shy Anne's message, at least I didn't think so. Maybe he wanted her to talk more about fun and excitement, but for some reason didn't just ask her. Instead he said, "We are looking for a night's stay. We're traveling and need our rest." Maybe he said that kind of off-target thing to smoke Shy Anne out, make her talk more plainly.

117

Shy Anne looked puzzled but stayed calm. "Like I said before . . . that will be quite expensive. Seventy-five dollars if you both stay the whole night and get the whole program."

Again her language threw me. Program meant a musical program or a sports program, or a religious program back in Sioux Center, and I couldn't see any of that taking place at Shy Anne's. So the idea of a program left me without understanding. Before I could ask she continued, "Now, if you stay for just an hour I can offer you a very reasonable price: ten dollars apiece."

I figured that was very expensive for a nap, and we would still have to find a night's lodging someplace, or we'd have to find a place to pitch our tent. But I realized I hadn't gotten what was to be in the program. I just hadn't gotten the full meaning of fun and excitement yet, but I was beginning to get the full picture.

I really had the facts of life fully brought home to me as two women came into the room and joined us. Shy Anne hadn't called them, at least I never heard such, but here they were. My attention to Shy Anne was destroyed right there, as these women only wore negligees! I knew it was awfully early to be dressed for the night, but I had to admit I didn't know the customs of Deadwood and these women might actually be ready to get their night's sleep. But in the back of my mind I doubted that, especially as sweet smelling perfume wafted to the sofa and they smiled in a pleasant way, just like one of Clark Gable's girls did, just the same comely way.

Shy Anne must have felt this charade had gone on long enough and spoke frankly but gently. I sat in admiration of her skill and decided that she was a master negotiator equaling any labor contract negotiator in Washington, D.C. "Boys, these two ladies will entertain each of you, separately, for an hour. The cost is ten dollars and you must pay first. We have very private bedrooms so you won't be interrupted or embarrassed." She paused and I felt the tension of the moment and wished I still had my suitcase to hold onto. But it stood by itself immediately before my feet and it didn't need any holding. But somehow or another I needed the holding.

Shy Anne continued in a whisper and I leaned forward to grasp everything she might say. "I don't know how experienced you boys are. I really don't." She paused, hoping Wes or I would answer, but when we failed to come forward she followed, "This might be your first time out, and if it is, you don't have to worry. These two ladies, Irma and Norma, are very gentle, though quite experienced. Please be assured you'll be in good hands and will make out just fine."

All my speculation about Shy Anne's program, about whether hers was a rooming house, came to a dramatic resolution, one about which I had clearly wondered, had some unexpressed hopes for, but one I could not face. Dodging its real meaning stemmed from my moral upbringing. My sexual yearnings were usually kept in the background. But Shy Anne's subtle persistence and the entrance of Irma and Norma had really reached them.

Shy Anne raised her eyebrows slightly, suggesting the time to make a decision was at hand. Irma and Norma smiled easily and looked at us in a kindly way. I thought Irma looked at me more than at Wes and I could feel a small but hot fire ignite for her. Her being older than I helped, rather than hindered, the fire. At first I could not understand it, but as I thought about it I guessed it was because she would test my manliness, and that was at stake here.

I was stimulated by what Shy Anne had said and found myself going for the deal in spite of its cost. Yet on second thought I knew that ten dollars was more than my purse could stand. It was a long way back to Sioux Center and the two remaining dollars after the ten dollars was spent wouldn't get us there.

Wes was a negotiator, like Shy Anne, and spoke positively. "I know it's worth it. As a matter of fact, worth much more than ten dollars, the beauty and manner of you all. But right now our money won't cover the fun and get us home. We've got a long way to go."

Though Shy Anne's face was clouding and Irma and Norma tensed in their chairs, Wes continued, "Might you consider something less, less than ten dollars?"

Shy Anne raised her eyebrows to show her distaste for the whole idea of bargaining over such a personal matter. "On such an important thing as intimacy, it's unfair and unethical to bargain." She was certain; however, her manner suggested she was still open to negotiation. I was a bit puzzled because I didn't know what intimacy was, but I figured it was sex. I was glad she used the word "unfair" because I knew all about that. But the word "unethical" threw me.

Wes, practical by nature, did not get involved in matters of ethics, which he must have considered a side issue, and simply asked, "What's your final price? Give it careful thought. It can't be ten dollars."

Shy Anne looked at Irma and Norma and they in turn sized us up. We tried to look impressive. We pushed our chests out, smiled and hoped to make a favorable impression, all to pass their evaluation. That is, we wanted to look so extraordinarily manly to make up for their loss from the usual take of ten dollars. We looked at them carefully, not quite pleading, but I think we must have had some of that in our eyes. But it didn't help, and they turned away from us, which meant it was all over.

Shy Anne picked up on their cue. She rose, came to the sofa, reached out and patted Wes on the head and quietly said, "I know you are for real, but I think we should look forward to next year. I'm sure you'll be coming back here again."

Wes continued to be practical. He knew the game was over, and thinking about his limited money he was happy to have found a way out of a situation that had become even too complicated for him. I was relieved but felt cheated. While Shy Anne gave Wes undivided attention as she brought closure to our efforts, she did not give me any. The only thing I had were my fantasies and several final affirming glances from Norma. I stood, picked up the suitcase and walked to the door. Wes had a thing or two more to say to Shy Anne. She must have liked what he said as she smiled broadly, the first since we had entered.

He joined me at the door and we retraced our steps down the stairs. When we reached the street we both looked up at the sign and I said, "I sure like that lace."

"To be truthful, I sure do too," Wes agreed.

"Their price wasn't too high, but there's no way we could swing it," I lamented.

"We could have volunteered to do handyman work for them. You know, whatever needed to be done around the place. And instead of getting paid we'd take it out in trade." Wes smiled as he spun out his thoughts. "I had thought of it, but I was afraid that would get more mixed up than we could handle, so I didn't say anything."

"Should have. Should have," I groaned as I recalled Norma's last glance at me. One that seemed to say, "I am sorry."

I said, "I wish I would have had that idea. I would have pushed it. Wes, if I were as smart as you, we would still be up there!"

"It's getting late," Wes observed. "Really late. We've got to get back to the service station, pick up our pup tent and ask the attendant where a good campsite is, with toilets and showers and a store close by. I'd like to repeat last night, get some steaks, roast them over the campfire. Repeat the whole thing."

The filling station attendant was helpful. "Sure. There's a good campground just about six or seven blocks up the road. It's a block or two off the main drag, so it should be quiet and safe. Go north for four blocks and turn to the right. You'll walk right into it after a couple of blocks."

We thanked him for keeping our tent and started for the campground. We encountered a grocery store en route. In addition to steak we bought a loaf of bread, a half dozen sweet rolls and milk too, for breakfast. "We can afford it," Wes estimated. "We must each still have about twelve or maybe thirteen dollars. That's pretty good when you think we started with about seventeen, and the distance we've come."

"Sure is," I agreed and felt comfortable with the estimate.

We entered the campground and found but one other tent in the area. The recreational vehicle part, however, was overflowing. "Just goes to show you," Wes admonished, "we're not up to date."

We laughed, found a great site for the tent located close to the facilities, but not too close. We didn't want to be bothered by the toilet and shower traffic. We pitched our tent in a hurry, cut

121

some roasting sticks for preparing the steak, gathered firewood and readied ourselves for the evening. As soon as it turned twilight we took a shower and returned to the site and started the fire. It turned to coals soon and we roasted our steaks.

The butcher had given us excellent cuts, as had the one in Belle Fourche. As we turned them over and over above the coals our appetites rose to a height as if we hadn't eaten all day. Once the steaks were roasted to the pinnacle of brownness, we pulled them from the fire and then from the sticks, using slices of bread as hot pad holders. Once the steaks were eaten, I suggested that peaches would really top off our meal and pulled a can from the suitcase, opened it and we passed the can back and forth between us until it was gone.

"Do you remember Miss Walsh giving us lessons on etiquette before we had the eighth grade banquet?" I asked, thinking back several years.

"Sure. Sure. She must have figured we and our families knew nothing about good manners, especially table manners."

"I think she really believed that, and that's why she threw herself into giving us that cram course before the end-of-the-year banquet. After all, we were graduating from grade school."

"So what do you think Miss Walsh would have to say about our manners out here, eating out of cans, two people eating from the same can? Sometimes with only one spoon! Eating steaks off roasting sticks and slices of bread, all with plenty of exercise with our hands holding the steaks, holding the bread, and all the rest of it."

"I fear she'd have a nervous breakdown!"

Wes slapped his thigh and laughed. "She'd figure her whole career had failed, was a waste, and that we so abused her teaching that she had the breakdown!"

"You're right. You're right," I agreed, and we laughed and laughed. But then Wes added a serious note. "She wanted our eighth grade banquet to be a success and she wanted to be sure all of us heathens knew which fork to use, and not to slurp our soup. So she gave us some coaching, which most of us really needed."

"I know. I know," I added. "She did okay. But we're not going by her rules now!"

We sat around the fire for an hour talking about our trip and speculated what it might have been like working on Tex Webster's ranch. We regretted there wasn't enough time left in the summer to do that. He was such a relaxed, fatherly person. We also wondered what those neighborhood girls were like, and the Saturday night dances.

We had had our showers earlier and after pushing our suitcase and shoes to the end of the tent we crawled under the blanket with our clothes and jackets on, ready for a cold night. Wes complained, "Gee, I hope it doesn't get as cold tonight as it did last night."

"I figured you knew what I was doing when I picked up a handful of old newspapers at the gas station. I put them on the floor of the tent so we won't get the cold from the ground."

"Yes, I saw you take the papers. They are a great help when things cool off."

Somehow Shy Anne hadn't come up in our conversation. Finally Wes introduced her. "Wasn't that Shy Anne something?"

I answered, "Wes, I've got to give you credit. First you moved ahead with Dot this afternoon and this evening you were keeping up with Shy Anne. Maybe keeping ahead of her. Showing her the way. You must feel pretty good about moving those negotiations a long way."

Wes challenged quickly, "Yeah, but we didn't make it. We never got into the real game. I still haven't cooled my fever for Shy Anne, though I would probably have had to settle for Irma, maybe Norma, whoever you would leave for me. I was all for Shy Anne, but I thought she only reserved her action for the town's leading customers and big spenders. That's why she had both Irma and Norma come in. She wasn't going to fool with us. If I thought we could make a deal I'd be for walking back over there right now."

I yawned, though my enthusiasm was as high as Wes's. "It just goes to prove we should have worked another couple of weeks before we made the trip. Then we could have talked business with Shy Anne."

"Dream about it," Wes suggested and turned over.

Chapter Seven
Days Six and Seven: Traveling and Criminal Justice

Excepting for the cold that woke us up occasionally, we slept soundly. We awoke stiff and climbed out of the tent into the sunshine. After dressing and a quick trip to the toilet, washing ourselves under cold water pouring from a park faucet, we pulled the wrapper off the sweet rolls and launched into our breakfast. We each ate three and passed the quart carton of milk back and forth between us. My only comment was, "I should have taken more papers from the filling station. We could have used them to cover us!" Wes did not respond but ate his rolls and drank milk in silence.

We were downtown at nine o'clock, caught a bus and began a tour of the town. Among the new things we learned was that there had been an "Old Bad Land" red light district in Deadwood that prospered in the early days. However, the guide failed to mention how such interests were covered now. We also saw Deadwood's Chinatown, an old railroad center and several abandoned gold mines. The casinos, which we had already seen, were pointed out, as was the Mount Moriah Cemetery.

We jumped off the bus at the end of the tour and walked to the edge of town in a few minutes. "We'll soon be in Lead. The claim is that Deadwood and Lead are twin cities. But the local version is small compared St. Paul and Minneapolis, very small," I added, "Lead is just over there."

Almost immediately an old Chevrolet truck chugged up the road and stopped beside us. It had MIKE'S SALVAGE painted on its front doors. Though clear, the painting looked unprofessional, as if an eager handyman had done it. The truck appeared like good salvage material itself. We knew this was a junk dealer, and not a very prosperous one at that.

A jovial, elderly man, perhaps about seventy years old, leaned out the front window and called, "I'll give you a ride if you boys will behave yourselves. But you have to convince me. Anything less and I'll leave you right here on the road."

Wes spoke immediately. "The only thing we have in mind is to get to Lead to sightsee. Maybe for the day. Then we're going back to Rapid City, eventually to Mitchell."

"Mitchell? God protect me. This old machine would never get us there. I have to be careful, treat it right just to get to Lead!"

I laughed and suggested, "It looks good enough for the trip to Lead."

"I hope you're right. Now, if I can trust you to do the right thing, you are welcome to climb in here with me and we'll get started."

"We won't cause you any trouble," Wes assured, and added, "We won't hurt you. All we want is a short ride."

Though it was hard to converse because of the engine noise and the complaining of the truck's gears, I shouted, "What's there to see in Lead? What are the high spots?"

"Before I answer that I want to know your names and where you're from. And I want to tell you I'm Andy Docken. Been in business here for more years than your ages. Yes, sir."

Andy Docken had a mild appearance in spite of his tough talk. His blue eyes, wrinkled brow and crows' feet around his eyes stood out above his receding chin. He wore a railroad engineer's cap on what appeared to be a bald head.

We answered his questions as quickly as we could, afraid of losing a ride. It was not an appealing prospect, as the truck bed was loaded with the carcasses of several wrecked cars and odds and ends of farm machinery.

After Mr. Docken heard us out he said, "You sound like you're okay. Turn the handle there on the door and get in. Bring your stuff with you."

We weren't sure that we would get started. The engine roared and the transmission of the truck shook as Mr. Docken tried to move it forward. After several broken tries, he was able to get the several parts of the truck to pull together and we were under way.

Once comfortable about the performance of his truck Mr. Docken turned to us. "Boys." he appealed, "be sure to stay in school and bear down on your studies. I've done all right, pretty good for me. Own my home. Have kept my kids in school. Got a wife who is satisfied with what I'm able to do. But boys, that's not enough for you. So I say stay in school and make something good out of yourselves." He nodded his head to affirm what he was saying. "Yes, I mean it!" He nodded as he began to brake the truck as it began its long decent into Lead.

"You asked about sights in Lead a minute or two ago. Well, the big thing is the Homestake Mine. Other than that are the casinos and houses where the girls hang out. Both places you should stay out of."

The ride was a short one. Mr. Docken dropped us off in the center of town, within walking distance of the Homestake Mine. We said goodbye to Mr. Docken and were pleased that he was proud of his achievement. The truck complained terribly but finally got it together and pulled out of its tracks and moved down the road.

We said no more and went to the Homestake Visitor Center, passing many gambling places on the way. I recalled Wes's venture in Deadwood, wondering whether he might try another casino, especially if it had a beckoning hostess at its entryway, but he didn't make such a move. I was disappointed, because I would have liked making another try to engage a gaming table hostess in conversation and maybe more. I felt I had run into a poor prospect yesterday and was ready to make a new try.

The visitor center at the Homestake Mine was first class. That is, it was lodged in an attractive building with shiny glass windows and doors. Pictures of early-day mining covered the walls. The center's lighting was gauged to make them most realistic. The receptionist welcomed us and encouraged us to see a film on mining, especially at Homestake.

We entered a small theater along with other tourists and saw a professionally prepared documentary that showed the earliest techniques and current technology of mining. We marveled at the progress from early efforts to modern procedures. Precise drilling, blasting, moving the ore onto electric rail cars and extracting the gold from the ore were all covered. After the film an elevator took us into the mine and to a tunnel that was not being worked at the time. It gave us a clearer picture of gold mining.

Once we were back on the surface we returned to the street, each carrying a handful of literature on the mine, but not gold. "That was the real thing," I remarked and Wes agreed.

"I see the Gold Owl across the street. Looks like a hotel we could spend the night in," Wes mused.

"Right," I agreed. "All we need is money. They have restaurants and a casino too."

"This town sure has the flavor of the Wild West, like Deadwood. Both towns are surrounded by a dense forest that looks black from a distance. I guess we should expect it. It's a part of the Black Hills," Wes said as we walked along.

"You know, we never had a chance to say anything riding with Mr. Docken because of the noise but the streams and lakes were great to see," I commented and then added, "And there was a great canyon in there too."

After walking a ways further, I asked, "I don't know if you are interested, but there was a sign back there pointing the way to the Black Hills Mining Museum. It advertised having exhibitions of working mines, a life-sized model of a mining town, the whole thing."

"Sounds good," Wes said. "I saw the sign too, but there is a charge. So I doubt that we'll want to see it. We've had one mine tour and that may be enough."

I nodded and we continued walking up the street without a goal. We stopped in our tracks when we saw a huge cut in the landscape, an open space where a whole mountain had once stood but was scooped away in the search for gold.

"I know gold is valuable," Wes asserted, "but I don't think the whole earth ought to be destroyed in mining it."

"That's just you talking," I challenged. "I'll bet you would have a different story if you had a chance to get any of it."

He decided I was right and dropped the argument.

We looked around the beautiful setting of mountains and trees. I ventured, "I wouldn't mind camping out tonight but I'd rather get back to the Evans dorm. How do you feel? What would you like to do?"

Wes hesitated for a moment and said, "I'm for going back to Evans'."

With that decision we walked to the edge of town and began to thumb. "We've got all afternoon to make about forty or fifty miles. We're that close to Rapid City."

A recent Plymouth, a highly polished black sedan, stopped and the kind-appearing man behind the wheel introduced himself. "I'm Reverend Jason and this is my wife Ruth, and Bill and Ralph are in the back there." We looked, seeing two bright, appealing boys, perhaps six and eight, wondering why their father had stopped. "We're vacationing here in the Hills and are on our way back to Rapid," the Reverend said.

Hearing that, we quickly replied, "That's where we're going." We hoped the good Reverend would give us a lift.

Instead, he asked about us and our trip. We expected the inquiry to be part of his looking us over to determine whether he felt safe with us. However, this continued for some time and I wondered whether it was in lieu of the Reverend making a visit to one of his parishioners.

In the meantime, several cars passed us and we felt opportunities were slipping away, and thought the Reverend ought to pick us up or get on his way. Our pressure to get a ride brought the question to the fore directly. I asked, "Might you consider taking us into Rapid with you? We'll take up very little room, as little as possible."

The Reverend's solicitous attitude changed to matter-of-factness. "I'm afraid we really don't have the room. Sorry."

We were put out, especially since he had engaged us in conversation beyond the usual "Can I trust your kind?" His wife, Jane, had even asked about our families and whether we attended church, all of which struck us as strange. But we put up with it, figuring we would eventually be given a ride. So I asked again, "Might you consider taking us into Rapid City with you?"

The Reverend's matter-of-factness turned to firmness. "No, I'm afraid not. Sorry."

By this time we were annoyed and moved away from the car. Wes saw another car coming and had begun to thumb it, suggesting that we had had all the friendly conversation we needed and indicating what we really needed most was a ride. The Reverend pulled away, bidding us farewell. We did not respond because we were angry. For him to turn us down was okay. That was his business. But why stop, talk to us and pretend that he might give us a ride and then turn us down when other cars were passing us?

Wes charged, "I didn't have anything more to say to him. He pretended like he'd give us a ride, wasted our chances to get a ride with somebody else while he carried on. There were other cars going by us as he held us in talk."

I joined in the complaint. "If he's any judge of people and what they'll do, he ought to have figured out we would not hurt them."

"We could have doubled up in back with the two kids. That would have been okay."

I furthered the idea. "One of the kids could have sat in front. There was plenty of room up there, and that would have left the back for us and one of their boys."

"What else can we say? Nothing. We'll just cross that experience off because we've had such a good time out here."

As we were still complaining a small delivery truck stopped and a young fellow our age called out, "I'm just going up the road a ways, about five miles, to Silverton. It might help you to be there instead of here. More cars."

We shouted, "Sure," tossed our luggage into the bed of the truck and climbed into the cab.

"I just ran some deliveries of auto parts into Lead and I'm on my way back. I suppose you're on your way to Rapid City."

We nodded, skipped other small talk and asked, "Are you in school during the regular year?"

"Oh, no, I graduated last spring. I don't know what I want to do for my life. I'm doing this job, and will do it for a year. Then I'll make one move or another, maybe to college."

I was interested in learning what kinds of things he was thinking about doing. However, we came to the end of the trip shortly. "This is where I cut off," he announced. "I haven't helped you much, but the best of luck to you. You're on the right highway for Rapid City."

We jumped out, retrieved our luggage, and away he went.

"I wish we could have learned his name," Wes commented.

"No time for that," I said, and Wes put up his thumb to a passing car, but it passed us. There was one some distance behind it and we routinely thumbed it. Then a police siren went off. We were shocked. It was a state highway patrol car. It pulled up beside us and a tall, well built, stern man called out, "Where are you fellows going?" His broad brimmed hat, in the style of a Marine Corps campaign hat, stood out as he grimaced and beckoned us to his car with an authoritative finger.

As the siren finally stopped making that awful noise, I answered, "To Rapid City."

He listened closely, showed no reaction and demanded, "Where are you from and what are you doing out here?"

Again I answered quickly, showing proper respect for his position.

He frowned and was not impressed with my answer. "You know we don't like hitchhikers, not after what happened last month." He said the latter with emphasis and his heavy frown became deeper.

I tried, "We aren't doing any harm, and love South Dakota more than any place. We are trying to see it."

I felt my answer was adequate and that he would be on his way, perhaps after giving us a warning of some kind. However, he was not appeased with my explanation. "What you've told me is not convincing. You are on the road without transportation and you're soliciting rides. You don't have any employment that I know of. I'm turning you over to the local police in Silverton. They may charge you with loitering and vagrancy. They have the authority to do both."

"Officer, we're sorry, really sorry. We haven't done anything wrong, haven't bothered a soul, and surely don't intend to." I pleaded our case, but in vain.

The officer was short and to the point. "One of you get in the back seat, over there, not behind me, and the other can get up front with me. Throw your stuff in back."

Shocked, we were off to the local police department. Our good spirits of just a short time ago dropped to anxiety and fear.

The highway patrolman concluded, "I don't know what brings you here, but sightseeing is not enough, especially as hitchhikers. You don't belong here. You ought to be home working, especially this time of year, with harvest and all. You don't belong out here cluttering up the scene for the tourists. Besides those basics, I don't know what kind of nonsense you might have been up to. There have been a couple burglaries here. I'll let the local police check you out."

We didn't respond, as we figured such was useless and feared angering him. Our hope now was with the local police.

He continued, "I'm clearing you off the road. That's my job. I'll tell the locals clearly what to do with you. They may not like it, but I'll tell them just the same."

We did not like the prospects, but felt the local police could not be any worse than this stuffed shirt who either did not understand his job or was taking a small part of it too seriously. With all of the speeding and lawlessness on the highway, what in the world was he doing badgering a couple of teenage kids who had absolutely no malicious intent? But he was clearly in charge, so we rode to the police department without further objection.

He turned on the car's siren as we approached the police station, running it a full minute. He apparently expected some local cop to come charging out of the station to help him with a couple of desperados, hard core cases who had committed armed robbery or murdered a child or an elderly person.

No local cop came out of the building, to say nothing about running. Indeed, not a thing happened. The highway patrolman was indignant and cursed under his breath. "This bunch of choir boys don't know where the action is. Don't know where the authority rests."

I seriously wondered what action he was talking about.

For emphasis he grumbled, "I guess these fellows are inside sitting on their backsides drinking coffee. So let's move out! Bring your gear." He extended his right hand onto his massive .38 caliber pistol, suggesting serious consequences if we were to run.

We followed his directions completely, walked ahead of him and entered the station. An officer behind the first desk drawled,

"Clem, I heard your siren and wondered what the hell you were up to. Figuring from the past, I decided nothing important. I knew you'd eventually show yourself, and you have. Now what can we help you with?"

Clem was not put down. "You know the governor has urged hitchhikers to stay off the roads, and I personally believe he's right. I've got a couple right here, flagrant types. I recommend you crack down on them, set an example, put a damper on them. I don't want to see them on the road again. No way."

The officer behind the desk ignored Clem and turned to us. "Boys, I'm Officer James and I want you to pay attention to what Clem has said. He patrols the area and won't take having you back on the road."

I felt like he was giving Clem some much sought-after support, but was unsure of what it meant for us. We listened to Officer James carefully, being sure to accord him full respect. He gave full consideration to Clem, being more servile than before. "Clem, do you have a written report on these fellows? The details of your charge, what the kids did and where they are from? You know, Form 89. We need it if we press any charge, in fact to make an arrest. It's a pain in the ass to fill out but we gotta have it. I said about all I can say on that. Clem, you know all of that better than I do. It's an official requirement."

Clem ground his teeth and frowned. "My charge is loitering but I'm not fillin' out one of those damned forms. I'm too busy. My charge sticks even though it's verbal. You can hear me, can't you?"

He continued to exclaim. "Being out on the road is a serious matter. Even the governor and the legislature are heated up about it. All of that heat comes down the line, right down to me. But no, I don't have anything else on them. Sure enough you can take my word on it. They were loitering. They are vagrants. They are a public nuisance. I've done the responsible thing, I've delivered them to you. You don't need all of that paperwork. You just need to get ahead with it."

Officer James extended his jaw and pushed back in his chair. "Without a formal statement from you, we are limited in what we can do. You can appreciate that. We need a form, not words."

"If you're afraid to arrest them or take them into court because you don't have a Form 89, I think you're chicken. But I'll leave that up to you. The very least you can do is to hold them until you check with local businesses for any unreported shoplifting or bigger crimes, and check the crime reports for the area so you get a rundown on that. It could be these kids were mixed up in something and you should hold them until you clear them. Besides, you need to get in touch with their families or responsible person. All of that takes time. Let them sweat it out."

Clem's temperature went up as he talked, and finally he shouted, "You gotta put some heat on them. If nothing else, you might send them down to the work camp for a few days."

As I watched Clem thrash around in his anger, Shorty Hertz came to mind. They seemed so much alike. And I wondered if by some chance they had gone to the same school, that is, if they had gone to school at all. But I was afraid of both. Yet there was a difference between them. Clem had more authority and was more ready to use it. As I was sweating out our present trouble I was convinced that Clem was really bent on making it as tough on us as he could. In Mr. Hanson's class we had learned that along with many good policemen were those who, in fancy language, were the personification of public vengeance, meaning they were the public accusers of fellows like us, without a shred of humanity. They represented the law and justice and would do everything in their power to bend them in their will.

His eyes, like those of a lion, gazed directly down at me, down because he stood tall above me, and his expression was menacing. The campaign hat which was perched on his head showed his full authority.

Exasperated, Officer James offered, "Just leave them with me, Clem. I'll talk with them and then with Oscar when he gets back. Sure, we can hold them for questioning, but you know there's a time limit on that. We can't send them to the work camp. It's a penal camp. You can't co-mingle juveniles and adults. The camp is a mini-prison for adults. Clem, you're telling us to bend the law, if not break the law. You know that."

Clem straightened his impressive campaign hat. "I'm just telling you to do something that lets these fellows know they can't be hitchhiking in my area. I'm serious about this." Clem left, slamming the door behind him.

Our heads whirled as Clem listed alternative ways of dealing with us. Our fear mounted as Clem left and Officer James continued to extend his jaw back and forth as if it was on some type of mechanical rotor, and finally asked, "So, what are you doing out here? Where do you come from and where are you going? What's most important is, have you been into any stealing? Any shoplifting?"

His voice, while firm, did not have the metallic, cutting ring of Clem's. We explained ourselves in detail, even beyond Officer James' interest. The detail and emotion annoyed him but we showed our sincerity and, hopefully, innocence.

He repeated, "Have you been into any stealing?"

I raised my voice without being aware of it and shouted, "No! No way! We've been hitchhiking, that is true. We haven't hurt a soul and we sure haven't done any stealing. We know better than that!"

After hearing us out, he bluntly asked, "What am I going to do with you? I can't just put you back on the road or Clem is likely to pick you up. Then there would be hell to pay. Our jail isn't fit for detention, at least not youth, and the work camp is for adults, not kids."

As he screwed his mouth around, I urged, "Just let us go. We'll get a Greyhound back to Rapid. We haven't done anything wrong. We'll get out of your way."

With the threat of being locked up, the bus fare was not a consideration. We could easily afford that.

He seemed to ponder the possibility but frowned, shaking his head. "I'll have to lock you boys up until Oscar comes back. He's the Chief. I'll let him decide."

What we hoped would be a reasonable man turned to the opposite. Boiling with indignation he pronounced, "There's no way you're going to weasel your way out of this. No way." As he rose from his desk his enormous size became apparent. Little of it had shown before as he sat behind his desk. "Follow me. Leave your stuff out here."

We had been conciliatory, but the threat of jail provoked me. "Look, you can't hold us without an arrest, and you can't arrest us because you don't have a real charge. Clem wouldn't issue one. I don't know why, but there is a reason for that. You're not locking us up. No way."

I didn't know if what I said impressed him or the defiant way I stood. At any rate Office James reconsidered his threat. Whatever knowledge I had about the ins and outs of an arrest came from my ninth grade civics class with Mr. Hanson, who saw himself steeped in the law. He had talked about the rules of evidence and the required procedures for an arrest. Officer James was violating all that Mr. Hanson had told us.

My blurting out did intimidate him. "Okay. Sit with me until Oscar comes back." Though still in a panic, I felt strengthened from our victory and I thought Wes was too.

Oscar returned about an hour later. He was a square-faced man with the wide shoulders and deep chest of a truck driver. He wore his uniform smartly and walked with a swagger, and there was something belligerent and indomitable about him. His eyes were brown, darker than usually seen, and his mustache was shading black to gray. He listened to Officer James' report, intermittently rubbing his head and scowling. He sized us up but otherwise paid no attention to us. His mind was obviously on other matters.

Finally, facing Officer James he called out, "You need to know a couple of things. First, I've got a headache over a personal problem—Frieda is leaving me and I was over to see Ted Belk at the bank. As you know, he's the head of the local party. He told me that they won't back me for mayor unless I can show some aggressive law enforcement. The kind the voters can get behind."

Officer James did not comment and we remained quiet, feeling the Chief's revelations were out-of-bounds for us. I figured he was so worked up that he talked in spite of us.

"Frieda said she couldn't take the loneliness of being an officer's wife any longer. Too many nights alone, too many worries."

Oscar became aware of the inappropriateness of his remarks before us, and focused on Clem. "Now what the hell is the matter with Clem, pushing his authority, bringing these kids in here and telling us what to do. He gets on my nerves. The next time he comes in here without a Form 89, I'll occupy him and you go out and deflate his tires. Then we'll see how well he handles a real problem." Oscar laughed and slapped his thigh. "I don't want you to forget it. We'll do it just as sure as we're sitting here."

He laughed heartily in his self-indulgence, then returned to us. "Now we have a couple of kids with us." That he was bearing down on us was clear. "So Clem picked you up hitchhiking?"

We nodded. I quickly added, "We weren't doing anything wrong. We weren't hurting anything."

The Chief's impassive expression didn't change, making me very uneasy. In fact, it made me feel worse.

"One of you, only one, come into my office." He pointed at me. "I want to talk to you." I followed him.

The Chief turned and shouted at Wes, "I'll see you later."

The brightness of his office caused me to lower my head, and as I sat in the chair indicated by the Chief, I realized the exceptionally bright light was shining directly at me, like a spotlight. I felt like I was about to get the third degree. Just like I had read about.

The Chief seated himself behind an exceptionally large desk. His foreboding appearance was reinforced by a pair of handcuffs mounted on an oak plaque that hung behind him. The printing underneath the plaque said, OUTSTANDING POLICE OFFICER OF HILL COUNTY 1935.

He folded and unfolded his hands several times, and his scowl deepened. Along with licking my lips, which were very dry, I squinted as the light bothered me. I hated the guy's guts and asked, "Might you turn down that light, or off altogether?"

He raised an eyebrow, surprised by my request. The Chief shook his head and continued his silence. I knew he was trying to scare me, so I kept my cool, sat there and said nothing. Finally, without a change of expression and hardly moving a facial muscle he asked in a monotone, "Why are you and your friend roughing it out here?"

"Sightseeing. Seeing the Black Hills."

"How long have you been in this area?"

"Three or four days."

"How have you been traveling?"

"Hitching it," I replied, though knowing it might do us in.

"Are you sure you and your pal haven't been into anything else—shoplifting, burglary or something worse?"

I gave a negative shake of my head but did not answer otherwise.

The Chief pondered my response and I felt he accepted it. "We'll have to check any reports of crimes in the area. Where have you been? What towns?"

I answered quickly. "Deadwood, Spearfish, Sturgis, Belle Fourche and Lead," I said, adding, "I don't know what's happened there, but you can't hold us for something we didn't do. We did not commit any crimes any place along the line."

"Just let me handle it," the Chief ordered. He eyed me like a vulture. His eyes gazed intently. He carried his stare with arrogance. Leaning forward a little, the better to dominate me, he seemed to be saying, "Look, I've just started with you. If you think you can get away from me, you're sadly mistaken."

Finally he spoke again. "Now I want you to fill out a piece of paper for Officer James, giving your home address, name of your parents and that kind of thing. We may want to contact them. And if you have any relatives in the area, just write that down too—somebody who can vouch for you. That will be all for now."

As I rose and walked out of the room he added, "This investigation will take a while, just to check you and your friend. So don't be in any big hurry to get away."

Frightened by the possibilities I challenged, "You can't hold us without an arrest, and you can't hold us without clearing it with a judge."

"Let me deal with what I can and can't do," the Chief growled. "Now send in your partner."

Upon entering the outer office, I filled out a form for Officer James. I considered not cooperating but decided such would only make matters worse. I perked up when I reached the question,

"Do you have any local contact?" Mr. Evans came to mind. I felt he would help us. Yet I hesitated to enter his name and address, not wanting to be a bother. Further, I felt it embarrassing. But the bottom line was, we needed help and he had the prestige to help us. I entered his name and address, and underlined them.

Officer James got up, got himself some coffee. Though somewhat smaller than the Chief, he too was ponderous, probably six feet four or five inches tall and around three hundred pounds. He sighed as he sat down. "Doesn't make sense, you and your buddy running around when you have a home in Sioux Center. There must be work to do back there, harvesting and all."

I explained our adventure but it fell on deaf ears.

"You'll have to open your suitcase and other stuff so I can see what you have. Later I will have to search you to see what you are carrying in your pockets." He saw my anger rise and commented easily, "Just routine, just routine. I've got to do it."

I called his attention to Mr. Evans' name as the tension built. He nodded but made no reply. I had half a mind to give him Mr. Hanson's name as a teacher at the high school but gave that up when I realized he was on summer vacation and away from Sioux Center. I enjoyed the thought as I envisioned Mr. Hanson tackling Officer James. It would not have been a match. Mr. Hanson was too smart. But then I realized Officer James had the real power. Further, the whole idea was fantasy.

I pulled our suitcase open. Officer James exclaimed, "What in the hell have you fellows been doing? Stealing groceries? Pilfering from grocery stores? Shoplifting?" His hilarity changed to gruffness. "So, come clean. Where did you fellows steal that stuff? Whose shelves did you lift?"

Defensively, I explained. "From our pantries back home. Wes's father drives a truck for the Raven Brothers. He buys these things wholesale. He bought what is in the suitcase."

"That's a fine story," Officer James scoffed, "but it doesn't hold water."

I countered, "It's the truth."

Officer James ignored me. Then he asked, "What in hell is this tent for?"

139

In exasperation I explained, "That's what we've been sleeping in. Brought it from home. We've been sleeping in public parks."

Officer James discounted my explanation. "Do you want to empty your pockets or do you want to wait until later?"

I stood my ground. "I'll wait. Besides, there's no need for it."

"Sit down until Oscar finishes with your pal. But in the meantime, not later, empty your pockets, especially your money, and I don't want you carrying any weapons. That includes knives."

I was ticked off at him and this whole situation and just said, "I'll wait."

"You can't wait because I'm saying do it now."

Officer James was so heated I followed his orders and quickly. I was afraid of being struck. I poured $13.25 onto the table and a badly used handkerchief. My jackknife was included.

Officer James raised his eyebrows. "I'll put all of this in safekeeping for you. I'll write the items on the envelope so you can check it when you get them back."

He saw the anger on my face and explained, "Don't worry. Nobody will steal them. You'll get it all back when we let you go."

I bent to his demands and he put my $13.25 and the knife in a big brown envelope and I sealed it.

His only comment was, "We'll have your friend do the same thing when the Chief releases him."

"Why don't you contact Mr. Evans?" I urged. "He'll tell you we're okay. He'll tell you we can be trusted. He'll tell you we've done no wrong. None."

"We'll wait and see what the Chief has to say." Officer James returned to a stack of papers on his desk.

I sat down and saw our being held as going on and on, and I was unclear as to when it would end. And whenever that might be, it wouldn't be good.

I waited and waited, wondering what the Chief was doing differently with Wes than he did with me. Finally Wes came out of the Chief's office followed by the Chief. Wes rolled his eyes and raised his eyebrows, which I thought to mean the interview was out of this world, and we were in for a rough time. "James," the Chief pronounced, "come in. We gotta talk this over."

Wes sat beside me. Neither of us spoke but shared the same dismal feeling about our future. We waited nearly an hour, at which time the Chief and Officer James came out. The Chief stood over us and talked in the combined style of "Father Knows Best" and that of a deliberate, stately judge. "Boys, we're holding you overnight for further investigation, and if we don't get two things cleared up, I'm sending you to the work camp over at Windom. The two things are: are all these groceries yours, or did you shoplift them, and I've got to get back to Clem on this loitering charge. There's no ifs, ands or buts about these matters. We have to protect our communities and we must clear the road of hitchhikers."

I jumped up, shouting, "This isn't fair! We haven't done anything wrong, haven't hurt anybody and we weren't loitering."

"I'll follow up on the Evans reference, but you are going to spend the night in lockup."

He lightened up a little. "If we're going to keep you, we have to feed you." He turned to Officer James. "Take them over to Ted's and get them the blue plate special. It's past lunchtime."

We followed Officer James to a police car and in a few minutes we were parked in front of what looked like a working man's cafe. "Follow me," Officer James ordered. We entered the cafe, seeing it nearly full of families having dinner. Officer James pointed to the counter. We took a couple of seats. Officer James sat beside me and without looking at the menu ordered. "Three blue plate specials. Give me coffee and give these two fellows milk."

The meals were served in short order. Without hesitation we all moved to eating. Nothing was said during the meal excepting Wes's comment, "This beats eating beans!"

Officer James talked quietly with the cashier on our way out. We knew it was about us, as the cashier looked at us several times during the conversation, but we could not hear what was said. We drove back to the jail in silence. I considered bounding from the car but felt it would be fruitless, and furthermore, I might get beat up in the effort.

"I'll put you in lockup now," Officer James announced as we entered the building. Dejected and defeated we followed him down the hallway. He unlocked the outer door with a huge key and ordered, "Keep moving."

I walked reluctantly into the cell block. It was quite dark, as only a limited number of lights shone in the whole area. They hung from the ceiling in the middle of a walkway that extended from the doorway to the end of the unit. There were eight cells on each side of the walkway. Once my eyes adjusted to the darkness I saw the whole cell block was painted gray: the floor, the walls and ceiling. The cells were framed by bars. Each had a toilet, sink and a mirror made of stainless steel which only vaguely reflected the image in front of it. Everything was exposed. There was no privacy anywhere. An officer could survey the whole unit from just inside the door. A flashlight might help; however, the view was open to him. The place had a bad smell, like that of a urinal and toilet in a poorly run service station, and though there was a large fan fastened to the front wall, it was at full rest.

Before I got my full view of the place Officer James growled, "I'm putting you," he said, pointing to me, "in here."

I hesitantly entered the cell and sat down on the iron framed bed, which was attached to the wall. Springs were still to be introduced into the affair. Instead, there were heavy gauge metal strips that crisscrossed the frame, and a thin mattress was doubled over the frame. A couple of sheets and a blanket were folded, resting on top of the mattress. No pillow was in sight.

"Now I want your shoes," he ordered. "I already got your friend's. Make yourself comfortable and I'll get you up in the morning."

"How about supper?" I demanded.

Officer James shrugged. He motioned to Wes. "I'll take you down to the other end and you'll have the same situation. I don't go for talking. So you boys will be hard put to do that. Your cells are too far apart."

The door clanged shut with Officer James' force. He locked it and was on his way to do the same for Wes.

I walked to my bed and lay down without taking my clothes off. I wondered whether it was really true that we were locked up. But we were. I wondered about my sister and family at home. I wondered how the various people were that had given us rides and treated us so well: Mr. Jenkins and his smelly chicken truck; Mr. Jackson from the state reformatory and Melvin, the runaway; Bill Reston and his work with the Sioux Indians; Mr. Adams and his retirement from twenty-seven years of teaching; Ken Collins and his appliance repair business; Dan Larson and his enthusiasm for his teaching career in the Kadoka; Otto and his future in picking up his studies at the School of Mines; Tex Webster and his ranch, and his son Todd hoping for success in his transfer to the School of Mines; Mr. Yates and his Campbell Soup sales; Bill Neal and his auto parts business; and Mr. Evans and his Stanley Steamer. I lay there with these pleasant thoughts and the phrase, "And this, too, shall pass," came to mind. My Uncle Albert had told me that as he put his hand on my shoulder at my mother's funeral.

I realized I had not covered all the people who had been so giving and kind to us.

I had deliberately skipped being picked up by Clem, the highway patrolman.

Officer James came back late in the afternoon with sack lunches which were our supper. A sandwich, an apple and a piece of cake were quite good. He brought a copy of *Sports Illustrated*. I nodded my appreciation but said nothing. He knew my view of our being locked up and I was not going to change that.

I ate the meal casually as I read the magazine. I continued to read in the evening. It calmed me down.

I figured it was dark outside now. A light though dim shone in the walkway of the cell block so the Chief and Officer James could see us. I stretched out on the mattress, put the magazine aside, put a folded handkerchief over my eyes and went over the details of our trip again and again.

I was drifting off to sleep when the sharp clang of the cell block door and clicking of the lights brought me to full attention. "Right over, here," Officer James ordered. "Right over here."

The new inmate nodded as James pointed to the cell next to mine. The man was middle aged, short and square. He had extraordinarily long hair and a deeply lined face. He wore unkempt designer jeans and a soiled sport shirt and jacket. This was topped off with a paisley silk cravat around this throat. His lazy eyes fastened on me and he followed with a "Howdy," like he might greet some one next to him at a local bar. "Howdy," he repeated as he continued to size me up.

The bright light went off and the cell block door clanged shut. Officer James was gone. I could see only the outlines of my neighbor as the night lights shone from some distance away. He followed his second "Howdy" with an easy, "Don't suppose either of us want to be here."

I agreed and he continued in a friendly way. "The criminal justice system always has its net out and its catch today was you, me and your friend down the cell block. . . . So, we're all here," he chuckled. "All here."

I wondered how he knew Wes and I were friends, but I didn't focus on it. I was too busy looking over my neighbor.

Slowly, but without missing a beat, he unfurled parts of his life history. "No, I wasn't much of a student. School and I didn't get along. Weren't suited for each other. When I got a chance, I quit. I turned to work, but I wasn't much there either. Did construction. Still do. You don't have to know anything to do it, the laboring kind. No, I'm not much of a worker. But I work at it."

He stopped and looked over at me, but no real eye contact was possible. Perhaps because I listened and didn't object, he continued. But it struck me as strange. Why would he do all this talking at the end of the day, and to a kid less than half his age? I reasoned that he was lonesome. Maybe had a few too many beers, or something stronger. Maybe. Then I ran out of ideas.

He talked on. "Now, son, you may not want to hear this, but I like to hang out at Smoky's, a local bar. I have friends there. We talk, share the gossip, watch sports."

"Sounds good," I murmured without interest.

But that did not put him off. Maybe he didn't read me. At any rate, he continued to talk about himself and then ask specific questions. "So, where do you come from? What are you doing out in this part of the country? More to the point, what are you doing in here, this of all places? You mean to say you and your friend haven't been shoplifting? Or anything heavier? Do you expect me to believe that?" He challenged me and I answered with vigor, giving him the full story.

He ended with, "Are you giving me the God's truth?" Though I had answered him fully, he repeated his questions about our being into shoplifting and other criminal things. I got an odd feeling that it was more like an investigation than a couple of cell mates sharing their experiences. I couldn't figure him out. He was nagging me, was annoying me. He had pushed his interest much, much too far.

To shut him off, I tried in a friendly way. "It's late. Let's talk more tomorrow morning." Then I shifted. "I've had it."

He didn't mind and simply replied, "If you say so."

I slept well in spite of the strange and hated surroundings. I peered at my neighbor the following morning and saw him reading a paperback, a privilege we had not been offered. He repeated his "Howdy" of the previous evening, and added, "I didn't hear you roll around so you must have slept well."

I nodded, trying to avoid conversation. I rubbed my eyes, stood and straightened my clothes. My neighbor, whom I now thought of as Mr. X, watched, and upon making eye contact said with the directness of a judge or a cop, "I'll only bother you one more time. Are you and your buddy really clean? No cheating on the law?"

Disgusted by the repetition and the indirect accusation on a matter that was none of his business, I burst out, "Hell no! And get off my back."

Mr. X chuckled. "Now, son, don't get mad. I believe you." He squirmed and moved the paperback to the side of his bed, fumbled for words and finally said, "Listen closely, because our time is short. That is, I'm not for real. I'm a plant. The Chief can't figure you guys out. So I was put in here to get to the bottom of your case."

He checked my amazement and said, "I believe you and I'll tell him so. The big thing is the Chief plans to run for mayor." Mr. X talked further. "He's a poor Chief, a bad Chief. So he needs to pump himself up, show strength."

I nodded and he climaxed his point. "He's going to strengthen his record by trumping up charges against you and your buddy. In plain language, he's going to make examples out of you and your friend."

His voice grew firmer. "Get yourself an attorney, insist on talking to your parents or a close friend. Choose the most powerful person you can get."

He had risen off the bed and paused to take a breath. He spoke further. "The time is short. Too short for me to explain myself to you, but I may be back tonight. That is, if I can convince the Chief that I can get more information from you."

Mr. X was going to talk more but the clang of the cell block door and the appearance of Officer James stopped everything. Officer James barked his orders. "You," he said, pointing to me, "wash up. And you," he added, pointing to Mr. X, "report to the Chief." He unlocked the cells and we followed his directions.

Wes came into the washroom shortly. "What the hell were you and that bum talking about last night? I couldn't understand you, but I sure heard enough to keep me awake!"

"Easy, Wes. It's a wild story. I'm not sure I believe it, but let me tell you."

When I finished telling the Mr. X revelation Wes shook his head. "I'll be damned. Mr. Evans looks like our best bet."

"Right. We'll have to see when we can make our strongest pitch."

Officer James put his head into the cell block and called, "All right, all right, let's move out."

We were greeted by the Chief, who was in a good mood. "Boys, I'm taking you out to breakfast, to one of the most popular places in town. A few of my friends hang out over there. I'll visit with them a little. But I don't want you to get nervous about that. Just go easy. And for sure I don't want you to get any

146

ideas about running off! You'll get your food just as fast as I can arrange it."

Overwrought, I shouted, "I told James and I'm telling you, we demand to see an attorney and talk to Mr. Evans!"

"Hold it there, young man," the Chief snorted. "Hold it there. You're not going to do either. They've got nothing to do with your loitering. Nothing! You're both going off to work camp. Count on it!" The Chief paused and put a smile on his face, but his voice remained gruff. "If you'll quit this stuff, I'll take you to breakfast."

I feared being put back in the cell, and nodded my head. I realized we would be on display in the restaurant and figured our tradeoff was good behavior for something to eat.

"Let's move out," the Chief ordered.

We went out the door and settled ourselves in his car. It was a shiny white one, having all the sirens and radio equipment that could be packed into it. I figured the operation of this equipment was probably beyond the Chief's capabilities, but I didn't challenge him.

Wes asked, "Is the restaurant you are taking us to supposed to be the busiest?"

"Oh, yes," the Chief responded enthusiastically. "You bet. One of the best in town."

"And we can have what is on the menu?" Wes queried.

"That's right," the Chief continued. His mood was good.

We stopped in front of a place called La Fonte Plaza. I didn't know what that meant, but it sounded good. We piled out of the car and followed the Chief into the restaurant. The Chief was immediately called a number of cheery, "Good mornings," "How are you?" "Haven't seen you in a while," and "How's it going?"

Somewhat in the character of a politician on the campaign trail, the Chief took off his police cap and whirled it on his forefinger as if he were ready to take the platform. "Fine, fine, boys. Just doing my regular job, protecting the public and preventing crime," he exclaimed to the group of five or six friends and nodded at us suavely. Wes and I stood resentful, and I knew it was baloney and politicking.

The Chief motioned to us. "Boys, sit over here." We moved into a booth and immediately took a menu. The Chief remained behind to talk to his friends. We listened but could pick up only a bit of what was said. It was clearly about us and his making an example of us. "Kids have to be kept off the highways," and, "Kids have to be disciplined."

We figured to hell with it, and selected the full breakfast entree and placed our order. The Chief delayed in joining us and in the meantime the waiter served us orange juice and cantaloupe. We disposed of that and were into Wheaties, strawberries and cinnamon toast when the Chief sat down. The waiter appeared quickly. "Make mine the regular, ham and eggs," the Chief ordered.

He gave the dishes before us a critical eye and imagined the amount we had eaten but did not say anything. We knew he was under public view and would not chew us out. So we asked the waiter, "Where's the rest of our food?" and clearly showed we were waiting for more. As the waiter puzzled, we ordered, "What about the ham and eggs, the regular?" He was glad for a further order and hurried off.

In the course of things, the Chief's ham and eggs were served and our ham and eggs followed. The Chief frowned when he saw our second breakfast arrive and sarcastically observed, "I'm damned glad I won't have you around for more meals."

We finished our breakfast without talking, and when we were in agreement, we rose from the booth and walked out of the La Fonte Plaza as proud as if we ate there every day, and the Chief waved to his friends.

As the Chief headed back to the police station he talked easily and was overly friendly. "I don't want you boys to get excited, but I'm sending you up to the work camp this morning. You'll probably be there a couple of days. That's how long it will take us to get this whole thing checked out. I can't keep you locked up while all of that is going on. When I get the evidence in I'll decide whether to refer you to the court or release you."

We began to protest, but the Chief raised his hand in the tradition of a traffic cop and we gave up.

We assembled our belongings when we got back to the station. Officer James said, "I've got them cleared for the camp, so as soon as we get organized we'll leave." He brought the envelopes containing our belongings out of the inner office and ordered, "Count it. Then we'll be set to go."

The money checked out okay. We nodded our heads and he said, "Let's go.

We, however, wouldn't move and I demanded, "What are we being sent up for and how long will we be there?" It was unreasonable and violated any sense of fairness. We stood our ground.

First the Chief tried humor. "Boys, it's like summer camp. You'll love it. You'll only be there a few days, maybe as short as a single day, just until I can get this evidence thing cleared up."

I resisted. "We didn't do anything wrong. And we're not going." We planted our feet firmly next to Officer James' desk. "We want to see an attorney, we want to talk to Mr. Evans. That's what we're going to do!"

The Chief changed direction. "You're charged with loitering and you're going to the work camp for detention. I can't be keeping you in jail. It just isn't the right place for you."

I did not agree. "Work camp isn't any place to be detained. That's a prison, and we're not going to prison!" My temper rose, and drawing on Mr. Hanson's class in civics I challenged, "You're breaking the law by denying us a chance to talk to an attorney or allowing us a chance to call our family or a friend. You're supposed to be upholding the law, not breaking it."

The Chief exploded. His face turned red and I could see the blood vessels rise on the sides of his head. Bitterly he ordered, "Boys, you better get into the car or we'll carry you in."

The Chief and Officer James stood over us and the Chief continued. "Get in, or I'll call two or three fellows to help us put handcuffs on you and put you in!"

We stood our ground.

"I'll be damned," the Chief swore and walked to the telephone. "Look, Murphy, could you spare a couple of fellows from the warehouse for about fifteen minutes? I have a couple of boys who need persuasion to get into one of my cars."

He apparently got an answer that he wanted, as he broke into a smile. He hoped to change our minds by just making the phone call and advised, "You still have time to get into the car."

But we didn't move.

In about ten minutes three of the biggest men I'd ever seen came in the door. "Well? What will it be?" The Chief faced us squarely. His voice had both a tremble and threat.

I knew the game was over and we had lost. I figured Wes did too. Carrying our luggage we slowly moved to Officer James' car. I sat in the front and Wes in the back. We were sullen, expressionless; neither of us spoke.

The officer methodically backed the car out of his reserved space, turned it slowly and drove onto the road. Before we left we heard the Chief thank the three thugs who had forced Wes and me into the police car. His face registered relief and achievement as he turned and walked to his office.

Officer James tried to salve our anger several times as we rode along, but we would not waiver on the basic wrong that had been dealt us. I mumbled to myself, "In no way am I giving in to James' cheap humor. I'm mad, justified in being mad and I'm staying that way." Wes seemed to be in the same frame of mind. So the atmosphere in the car was very frosty and Officer James felt it.

I didn't know how long we were en route, maybe a half hour, long enough for us to be approaching the work camp. Suddenly there was a sharp crackle on the radio. The Chief was on. "James, are you still en route? Where are you?"

"I'm just coming up on the gates of the camp."

"There's been a change in plans. I want you to return immediately. I don't want you to leave the kids. Bring 'em back."

"Oscar, I can't do that. Not after I leaned on the colonel to admit them. You know he didn't want to take them. Really resisted it, but I got him to do it and now I believe he's committed to it."

"That's all over with. Forget it. Turn your car around and come back."

"Oh, hell," Officer James grumbled to himself. "Why can't Oscar make up his mind?" He then answered officially, "Okay." But mindful of good relationships between agencies and the police, James drove on toward the camp. He had to make peace with Col. Newsome.

Wes and I had not spoken the entire trip, sitting depressed by our bad treatment. I was preoccupied with the work camp and our uncertain future. What was to become of us? We were startled and overjoyed by the message but dismayed by Officer James continuing on. I overthrew all reserve and challenged, "What the hell is the matter with you? Didn't you hear the Chief's orders? He said return, and return immediately, bringing us along!"

"Easy, easy," Officer James pleaded. "I've got to stop in and see Col. Newsome. He said he'd take you. So I have tell him that won't be the case. I figure it's best to tell him face to face than have a phone call or send a radio message."

We had heard the Chief's order and were certain that Officer James wouldn't do otherwise. But we were concerned about Officer James driving onto the camp in spite of the Chief's orders. Officer James' explanation was reasonable, so we finally relaxed and sat back in our seats as James drove off the highway into a long lane crowded by huge trees on each side. It was about a mile, and we wondered where we would end up. All of a sudden a large clearing and a line of military-like buildings appeared. We saw an administration building, dormitories, several sheds that must have housed tools and a large building that may have served as the mess hall and recreation center. Officer James stopped, jumped out and ran into the administration building. It was comical to see him run; usually he walked, and belligerently, to show threat and power. We enjoyed it and felt it was due to us.

We saw a formation of about fifty young men march into the camp's open space to the tool shed. They carried axes, picks, shovels and rakes. By command they lowered the implements from their shoulders in the manner of the army bringing their rifles to rest. When the officer in charge shouted, "Parade rest!"

the men left their tools on the ground before them and broke into small groups to smoke and talk.

Officer James wasn't gone long. He entered the building, running and came out the same way, jumped into the car, and baffled Wes and me with his remark, "I'm sorry to keep you waiting but just didn't want the colonel to feel like we didn't know our own mind on this. So the stop was worth it."

Given that it was clear we were the pawns in the whole matter, it should have been us to whom he was explaining himself, not the colonel. But if we were on our way to freedom, we let it pass. Wes leaned over, whispering out of Officer James' hearing, "I think it depends on whose advantage is being thought of."

Otherwise, the trip back to the police station was uneventful. We wondered what had happened to reverse the whole course of our lives. We knew it but did not understand it, but had a sense of relief and good feelings.

Officer James pulled up in front of the station, parked in his reserved place and announced, "We're back."

We responded by getting out of the car and following him into the station. We pulled our luggage along with us.

The Chief called out from his office, "James, I want you in here and the boys are to stay out." Officer James, wanting to know the reason for the complete change of direction, hurried in.

I was bursting with consternation and hope, and Wes put it into words. "I've been wondering what in the world happened to bring us back, and I even wonder more about what they are cooking up in there."

"It's gotta be good. It's gotta be good," I exclaimed. I didn't let the confines of the police station limit me any more. "It shouldn't be long and we'll know. Not too long."

Wes and I sat on uncomfortable chairs, wondering when we would learn the details of the new direction, wondering when they would break up and call us in. Listening carefully, we heard shouting, cursing and exclaiming, but nothing of substance, excepting, "What do we do now? What should we do with them? How do we cover our tracks?" Otherwise, the conversation was too muted for us to hear.

"We'll just have to sweat it out," I reasoned. "Just have to sweat it out."

"My God, it's taking them a long time to figure out what to do with us," Wes charged. "But on the good side, I'm sure glad they changed their minds about putting us into the camp. At least the Chief did. What I heard in Mr. Hanson's civics class was that what prisoners do to each other is bad, bad. They form gangs and sell protection. If you can't pay, they take it out in sex, homosexual sex. The guards don't do anything about it, as it helps them keep order, makes life easier for them. So rape goes on regularly. Couples pair off. All that kind of stuff. Besides that, the guards make life miserable for you."

I had heard that too, and countered, "They'd pay like hell if they tried that with me."

Wes agreed but added, "I don't know how well we could escape if a whole mob came after us." He shook his head in dismay but said nothing further excepting, "Jesus!" and rubbed his head.

I followed with, "That was a great course Mr. Hanson gave, but he got on the hot seat for some of the stuff he told us. Just like I'm telling you now. The complaint by some of the parents was that he was telling us stuff, especially things about sex, which they thought we shouldn't hear, felt we should be shielded from."

"I don't know that I blame parents for taking that stand," Wes defended. "You know the way things usually go back there in Sioux Center. That's the way to do it. Keep dirty things away from the kids. But when you get into a mess like we're in, what people in Sioux Center think doesn't count. No, it just doesn't count."

As we thought about the lack of connection between the ways of Sioux Center and the work camp, the door of the Chief's office opened. Officer James was the first to show himself. Even though we couldn't fully read the expression on his face, we figured it was foolish, just like a child who had been cheating in a final exam. He took the chair behind his desk. We sized him up as retreating, so different from his earlier self when he sat there as if ruling a fiefdom. His foolish facial expression then turned to defiance and anger.

The Chief's huge figure followed Officer James into the room. His step seemed lively and the expression on his face was amiable and pleasant. He sat on Officer James' desk, shading Officer James from our view. He began in a friendly tone, almost contrite. "Boys, Officer James and I have talked to all parties concerned, excepting Clem. We have checked all the crime reports and have not turned up a single thing which might be held against you. Not a single thing! What's more, I had a lengthy and heartwarming talk with your Mr. Evans. Let me tell you loud and clear, he's a gentleman, a real gentleman. The upshot of this very thorough investigation is that we are sorry if our detaining you has caused you any personal concern. It surely wasn't meant as such, just intended to be thorough investigative police work. Yes, thorough investigative police work. Now, I want to be sure your suitcases are intact, still carrying a full supply of groceries, that your pup tent is workable and that you have your full purse of money and your jackknife."

Though we had counted it before going to camp, we searched our pockets and checked it again. We looked at our tent and suitcases but did not inspect them. After we nodded, the Chief made the momentous statement, making me feel like the Fourth of July with all the rockets and flares going off and the local glee club singing "America." "Boys, you're free to go. I'm very sorry if we caused you any unnecessary grief."

If he knew the truth I would liked to have hit him on the side of his head with one of my hobnailed shoes. I, however, didn't try such, nor did we thank him, or even utter a word in our rejection of his phoniness.

The Chief broke the silence and suggested, "Officer James will run you down to the Greyhound depot and you can catch a bus to Rapid." He rose to shake our hands; however, we rejected his gesture and walked out of the door with Officer James. We all boarded the car. Our luggage, of which we had become fiercely protective, was up front with me and the officer.

He used the same light conversation as the Chief had en route to the depot. We shunned him, figuring, "To hell with you. We've had more than enough of you."

He stopped in front of the depot and concluded, "Goodbye." We did not turn or answer, but walked straight into the depot with our luggage.

Who should we meet when we got into the depot but Mr. X. He smiled and followed with his trademark, "Howdy." He spoke further, hoping to explain himself. "I figured you'd be here. I talked with the Chief this morning just after he checked you out with this man Evans."

"Why did he do that?" I asked. "He wouldn't bend on it before. I really pushed it but —"

"Well, when he first made the call, he figured on getting support to hold you. But then all hell broke loose! Evans told him in short order to release you or he would have the State's Attorney on his back. I don't know what else they talked about, but to butter the Chief up, Evans said he'd get the Chief on the annual program of the Dakota Law Enforcement Officers. This fellow Evans really can reach around."

I smiled and Wes did too. "I believe you," I admitted. "But how do you know all this stuff?"

Mr. X smiled modestly. "I thought you would have guessed by this time. I'm an undercover cop. Remember, I told you back in the jail. I became sympathetic to you because I believed you, and I knew the Chief could not be trusted. I urged the Chief to phone Mr. Evans. The Chief and I don't always agree."

With that he turned and walked out of the depot.

Chapter Eight
Remainder of Day Seven: Back to Rapid City

A quick check with the clerk told us that no bus would depart for Rapid City for a couple of hours. Wes picked up my feeling when he said, "To hell with all this. Let's hitch it."

We did and lined up on the edge of Highway 485 leading to Rapid City. Something we hadn't talked over before came up now. "What if Clem comes along?" Wes asked.

I responded, "What if he does? Well, I'll tell you one thing—old Clem is going to have one hell of a time taking us into custody. If ever I saw a phoney, he's it. But he damned near did us in."

Bravely we stood there thumbing, offering our best smiles as cars and several semi trailer trucks whizzed by and the drivers paid no attention to us. This had happened many times before. We were used to it. "I guess truckers will never stop for us," Wes explained. "If they did, the trucking companies would lose their insurance."

A few minutes later a trim looking Ford slowed to a stop. The driver asked, "You boys going to Rapid?"

We nodded with smiles.

"I don't know if I should be picking you up, but why don't you tell me your names, where you're from and why you want to go to Rapid. Can't be too careful these days."

"Fair enough," Wes answered and gave him a clear but short response to all of his questions.

The man listened closely and after satisfactory answers were given, he spoke. "I like your story. Sounds true. One of you get in front with me, the other in back with the luggage." He gave us time to get settled and announced, "Now we'll get underway. This car is just two years old. Got it when I retired. Figured I needed something steady, something I could depend on. I just drive around the area, see friends and relatives. No big trips."

I asked, "What did you retire from?"

In a short clipped way he answered. "Post office. Was a postal clerk. Right up at the counter. Like you've seen. Helping people with their letters and packages. Mainly selling stamps."

"Did you always do that?" I followed.

"No. No, no, I was a mailman, door to door for some years."

"Did you like that?"

"Like it is right!"

"How was that?"

"Well, if you boys take to listening I'll tell you all about it. You know people really demand their mail be delivered on time! They not only want the mailman on time but they like to use the mailman for all kinds of things. Now, it's not at all planned, you know. It just comes up by accident."

I urged him on. "What were some of the accidents?"

"Like on my last trip around the neighborhood some woman had washed a heavy rug. One of those hooked rugs, made right at home. Well, when it got wet it was mighty heavy. This woman needed help getting it out of the tub. Well, the two of us finally got it done, but in the meantime I got pretty wet. A fussy older fellow was waiting for me at the next stop. He looked at me, saying 'Cal,'—my name is Calvin Stevens—'Cal, what in tarnation did you get into? You look like you've either been sweating something awful or somebody has turned the hose on you.' Well, I made his day. He laughed and laughed. Couldn't get enough of seeing me miserable."

"So you've had some hard days?" I asked.

"Now, on having the hose turned on me, that actually happened a few times. Usually by kids. But not always. I had a few older fellows pull that trick too. One guy shot the hose on me as he came around the corner of his house and then claimed he hadn't seen me. Another guy shot the hose over the roof of his house and hit me. Small bungalows made that possible. They thought they were pulling a big practical joke. But to me it wasn't funny."

Cal's clipped language became even more so as he got excited about his past. "Yes, yes," he expanded, "there were bad dogs. You must know about them. Some people wouldn't call their dogs off. The dogs charged me, snapped at me, even bit me! Never saw anything like it. But I got back at them. Took some spray on my run and let them have it."

He laughed deeply. "Most owners couldn't take it and got mad. But I only laughed. Now there was one dog. . . . I don't know what his nose and lungs were like, but this spray didn't affect him one bit. The woman wouldn't do anything about him, and the dog kept coming after me, spray or no spray. I gave up and refused to deliver her mail. Let her pick it up at the post office!"

Mr. Stevens paused a moment, then continued without losing any momentum. "I took care of a lot of kids who were cut, scratched or fell out of trees, off the roof of a shed or tree house."

He rubbed his head and firmed his grip on the steering wheel. "You won't believe this and I don't blame you. In one case, I helped deliver a baby. The woman had waited too long to go to the hospital and there was nobody to take care of her. My first thought was to run back a block where I had parked my mail truck and drive her to the hospital, fast-like. But I quickly saw there was no time for that. I got her into bed, and when the baby began to come out I ran to the kitchen, washed my hands good, returned to the bedroom and helped her do the honors!"

Cal was living through these experiences. He tightened and loosened his grip on the steering wheel as he talked. The furrows on his forehead deepened and loosened and the pitch of his voice raised and lowered.

"These were trials for me, and no extra pay. The delivery did make the newspapers and the other mailmen kidded me about it, all in good spirit! I didn't mind. In fact, I liked it, but I didn't admit it."

Wes and I enjoyed the stories and Cal's pleasure in telling them. At the same time we saw vast expanses of hills colored by pines and wished we could take the time to do some backpacking. Not only would we enjoy it, but it would keep us out of harm's way, like Clem's law enforcement.

"Boys, we don't have far to go so I'll pass over some of the spicier parts of my experience. You're too young to hear them and I am too old to tell them. But just so you know what I'm about, it was my ins and outs with the ladies along my routes. Special ones, I mean. I got invited on the flimsiest excuses, and when I was new in the delivery business I took it just as they suggested it. You know, they'd asked me to move the bedroom dresser or move a kitchen or dining room table, or check the burner on the stove. Well, when I got into it, it didn't take me too long to realize they often had something else in mind, not lowering or raising a stubborn window, checking the thermostat or checking the vacuum sweeper. No, no, it wasn't any of that."

Cal stopped, leaving us in the middle of an adventure story, one in which we were seriously interested. I broke the barrier and asked, "What happened?"

"Boys, I can't tell you," Cal held out. "That is, I can't tell you how those times came out—the results. No, I can't tell you that, but I will tell you," he smiled very broadly before continuing, "I will tell you it had to do with what goes on in the bedroom." Cal slapped his hand on the steering wheel. "Yes, that's what it had to do with!"

Wes and I smiled and Cal could see we appreciated his adventures, though he hadn't described them fully. However, he fired our imaginations.

As Cal drove into Rapid City, he asked, "Where do you want to get off?"

"Evans Service Station," we replied.

"Great. I go right by there. You know, he's not only got a big business, but he's into public affairs. A real man's man."

We nodded and thanked Cal for giving us a ride . I added before closing the car door, "I am sorry we aren't riding with you a few more miles. That would give you a chance to tell your full story."

Cal laughed and drove off. As we walked into the service station I laughed and said, "You know, we didn't see Clem on the highway!"

There was a stir as we entered. We were quickly asked to join Mr. Evans in his office. He greeted us warmly. "So good to see you! What the world were you doing hanging out with police up there in Silverton? Really had to work on the Chief to release you. It took me a while to learn the right buttons to punch for him, but after I found them he became very reasonable."

We told Mr. Evans our whole story and nearly came to tears several times, especially when we felt trapped by the Chief without recourse.

"It's all turned out okay," Mr. Evans reassured. "Though I know you really had a tough time of it. Now what are your plans?"

"If it is all right with you we would like stay one more night and leave sometime tomorrow afternoon. We've read about the Prairie Edge Trading Company and Galleries, and would like to see that."

"You'll find it worth your time. Yes, by all means stay over to see that. You could easily spend up to three hours there. If you're in a hurry an hour will do."

We nodded and Mr. Evans concluded, "I'm glad you're safe and sound. If you need any help let me know."

We nodded again and thanked Mr. Evans for his help and left for the dorm. As soon as we reached our beds we dropped on them, feeling the aches run throughout our bodies.

"I guess we've about seen it," Wes observed as he lay back. "We came to see the Black Hills and we've seen them."

I nodded in agreement, a sense of satisfaction gathered in my voice. "It's been a great trip. After one more day we'll be on the road again. I would like to leave right now. We've been gone quite a while, about eight days. I'm really ready to leave, but while we are here we ought to see that trading post and art gallery."

Wes simply said, "I agree with you," and then added, "So how are we getting home?"

"After our run-in with Clem I'm for staying off the highways. I really am. I can't take another Clem, and even worse, another Chief. I don't like the freight cars but it may be the best way to go."

Wes nodded and shifted in his bed. "I'm really hungry. I didn't miss eating lunch until now, but now I really feel it."

I pulled cans of beans and peaches from the suitcase and looked over the supplies. "We're eating this stuff down. A few more days and we'll be out!"

"But so far so good," Wes added.

"Yes, thanks to your dad we are in good shape for several more days."

We followed our regular custom of passing the cans of beans and peaches back and forth between us until we finished them. Wes laughed and said, "I've said it before but it's still important. If Miss Walsh could only see us now! Manners aren't up to snuff, but we're getting along. Maybe she would excuse us because we are getting along!"

I suggested, "Let's just hang out here this evening, take it easy, get a good night's sleep, take in the gallery and that mercantile place tomorrow, and leave late in the afternoon."

"Good," Wes answered. "I've really gotten to like this place. The Rocky Miner on the wall over there is like a friend. I feel safe down here. Don't have to worry." He counseled, "Better get your math and science courses in hand, get your grades up and come out here to the School of Mines, and stay right here! Take the geology you've been talking about."

"Those are good suggestions, Wes, but I'm afraid they are over my head. At least I'm scared of them. I'll keep trying but I have to keep my feet on the ground on what I can do."

"Keep in mind that Shy Anne is just up the road and Norma and Irma too. They should be enough reason in themselves to come out here for your college work!"

"Oh yes, oh yes," I agreed. Then I turned a bit more serious. "Do you think we could have said something when we were up there that would have been more convincing? You know, have them want to spend some real time with us, not just talking and bargaining around?"

"I don't know about what could have been said, but what we needed was money. Not seventy-five, but maybe just fifteen or twenty extra dollars. They said ten dollars would be enough for an hour of sack time. But we didn't even have ten to spare, so we were out. And we didn't impress them enough with our looks to make them want to go to bed for just chicken feed."

"I didn't see anybody rushing the place. So why weren't they interested?"

Wes explained. "They have their pride. They must feel that anything less than ten dollars is below their standards, below what they feel they're worth. It's a feeling thing. I think that's probably the right word for it, but I don't know for sure."

"All that was new for me—being up there in Shy Anne's reception room—let me tell you. I wonder what the people in Sioux Center would think if they knew we were up there trying to get something like that for less than ten dollars! Even know we were just up there."

That set Wes laughing, which in turn started me off, and we laughed and laughed. Quips about Shy Anne's dress, jewelry and hair style kept us going for some time, long enough that tears ran down our cheeks. When we exhausted that fun we turned to Norma and Irma. Wes started it by, "You better write their names down so you can check them out if you come to school out here."

"Maybe we should leave the ladies for while," I suggested. "How about our not smoking? We haven't had a cigarette for over a couple of weeks. That's pretty good, I'd say."

"Yep," Wes replied. "But when the old Chief had us locked up I really could have used a couple. Maybe even more!"

"This traveling has broken the habit. But it's a tough way to do it. Anyway, it sure has worked."

"I think if we just keep our mind on football it will help too. We really want to make that team!"

"I wonder if the new coach is there yet."

"Probably is. Somebody told me he's going to recruit a couple of heavyweights who live on farms over by Elk Point. He's got a place for them to stay at Sioux Center. I guess they played at some church academy last year. Both played tackle and that's just what we need, some beef!"

Time passed and we felt drowsy. However, before falling asleep I said, "I often think about Mt. Rushmore, the beauty of the hills and herds of buffalo."

Wes mumbled, "Yes," so I knew he was about to fall asleep.

Chapter Nine
Day Eight: Last Day in Rapid City

We slept late the next morning, then showered, aiming to be clean for the trip. We washed our clothes, repacked our suitcases, dividing the remaining canned goods between the two, refolded the shelter halves and put all of this gear by the door. We left the service station and walked out into a sunny day.

Wes proposed what I thought was a good idea. "Let's buy some sweet rolls and milk and sit out in the sun and eat them."

We found a grocery store nearby and made our purchase. After some difficulty we found a bench on the street, sat down and, as bypassers looked at us, had the rolls and milk. In a manner repulsive to Miss Walsh we passed the quart of milk back and forth between us until we drank it all.

At first, curious bypassers bothered us. We thought they looked at us as if we were a new version of the American hippie. But as time went on we didn't care, as we were not concerned about the customs and manners of Rapid City and, as Mr. Hanson would have said to our civics class, "Not our priority!" In fact, we began to enjoy their second looks. It was part of experiencing the largest city we had been in. We saw their smiles as friendly, though curious.

"Did you say this place is at Main and Sixth in the Clower Building?" Wes asked.

"That's right," I answered. "There'll probably be a sign on the building."

After finishing our food we asked a passerby for directions and we were on our way. The walk took about fifteen minutes. We ended up facing a huge building posting an impressive sign: PRAIRIE EDGE TRADING COMPANY AND GALLERIES. We went inside and looked at the rich history of the area and tales of the past. We saw the crafts and arts of the Great Plains, a fine collection of photographs, oil paintings, water colors and pencil sketches. Though we had seen several similar exhibits, we were impressed nevertheless. We also saw a turn-of-the-century trading company, a book and music store and, of all things, an Italian glass bead factory. The overall emphasis of the place was that Rapid City was the gateway of the Black Hills. We didn't need any convincing at that point, but we were glad to see what they had. We left the building at mid-afternoon.

Wes commented, "It isn't a Mt. Rushmore or Homestake Mine or Sylvan Lake, but it was a nice place to wind up our Black Hills visit."

I nodded as we walked back to the service station, buying a large loaf of bread on the way. We planned to say goodbye to Mr. Evans and thank him for all of his generous help. However, he was not in. Luckily Otto Hoffer, the driver who had taken us to Mt. Rushmore and the area around it, was there. We talked to him, thanked him, wished him luck in his further studies at the School of Mines and asked him to thank Mr. Evans for us.

He said, "Sure. But why not write him a brief note?" He got us some paper and a pen. We followed his suggestion and put our best effort into it, gave it to Otto, thanked him again for showing us Mt. Rushmore and the other sights around it and went to the dorm.

After depositing the bread in one of the suitcases, we started for the freight yard. "Let's see if there is a train coming through. If so, we'll catch it. If not, we'll hitchhike," I said.

Wes nodded but was slow in doing so.

We were in the freight yards about a half hour later. "I feel kind of sad leaving," Wes muttered.

I answered, "I am too. So many great things. So many good people."

Shifting from the sentiment of our tour, Wes said, "I don't see anybody around to tell us about freights, but I'm sure somebody will show up."

He had no more than said that when a railroad man, probably a brakeman, came around one of the parked freight cars.

I asked boldly, "Any freights leaving soon? That is, for Mitchell?"

"There'll be one leaving in about an hour, maybe a little longer. Goes to Minneapolis but will stop in Mitchell to take on water and change crews. It'll get in there about seven tomorrow morning. Takes so long because the freight will have to park on the side tracks to let passenger and more important freight trains by. There's only one track."

We asked for details. "What track will it be on? How will we recognize it? Will there be any cops around?"

"Sure enough, there may be problems." He paused a moment and a cunning expression crossed his tan, sun-beaten face. "May be problems there, especially with the railroad cops. But if you boys could give me a small tip, I'll get you into a boxcar and away from the police. Then you won't have to worry."

We were vulnerable and he knew it. The upshot of the deal was his extracting a dollar from each of us for the promise of safety. We paid too soon, as no freight was in sight. Immediately after paying we recognized our error. He had our money and we did not have a box car. Afraid of being duped, we followed the brakeman closely as he checked the seals on cars and their numbers. His refusal to talk to us made us more suspicious.

"How could we have let him do that to us?" I said to myself. "We're tough but we don't know the ways of the world yet."

With our suspicions high, we followed him ever more closely. After a half hour of uncertainty he announced, "She's coming in now. Stay close."

We couldn't get any closer but knew what he meant.

The engine's brake screeched, its whistle screamed and steam hissed from its discharge valves as a huge train with a long line of cars finally stopped. Our anxiety mounted as the brakeman called, "Follow me." He checked several prospective cars but shook his head in each case, as the door was sealed. Finally we came to one that was open. He looked in, scanning the inside. "This one will be fine, plenty of paper if you get cold."

Wes and I threw our luggage in, jumped up and through the door and walked around inside, inspecting it. Though dim, there was enough light from the open door to allow our looking. We nodded our okay as the brakeman looked at us questioningly. He pulled the door shut part way and left. We expected the train to start rolling soon, if not immediately. However, it stood and stood, for an hour to an hour and a half. Our tension rose as time passed and we wondered whether it would ever leave. I sensed a familiar but unpleasant odor. "This smells just like the granary out on Uncle John's farm, kind of a sweet smell, but worse is that it is dusty." I rubbed my nose trying to help it adjust to the situation.

"I know what you mean. I don't like it, too full of dust. I guess we were too excited when we got in. But how we missed it, I'll never know."

I sneezed a few times and rubbed my eyes but my worry about the dust went away as the engine suddenly exercised its power, jerking the cars backward and forward and then moving ahead several yards. It was not pulling out. Rather, it was attaching more cars. We were nearly shaken off our feet but jumped around to keep our balance. The engineer did this for about a half hour as he built the train. Curious about what was going on, Wes and I looked out the door and were frightened to see eight or ten policemen with huge barking police dogs flood the yard. They checked the seals on the freight cars and peered into open cars. We hid behind a mountain of coarse wrapping paper, fearing being caught.

The train, which had been shifting around, stopped to accommodate the police. We huddled under the paper but could hear the police and the dogs clearly as they approached. Suddenly the car door was jerked fully open and a commanding voice shouted, "Okay, you in there, come out or I'll have a dog come and get you!"

Wes and I froze behind the paper. The cop repeated his threat. "Come out or I'll have a dog come and get you." This time his voice was menacing.

Stimulated by fear, sweat ran down my face and my heart pounded wildly. We lay still, without movement, absolutely quiet.

After a long pause, one in which we fully expected a snarling dog to jump into the car and chew us into bits, the cop backed off. "Oh, hell, there's no one in there."

Another cop agreed. "I doubt it. We've given it a good shot. Let's get on with the other cars. If there are a couple of kids around here, they are not in there."

Saved by their impatience, we breathed a sigh of deep relief. I whispered, "The paper saved us."

"Right. Then too, it's kind of dark in here. Their eyes weren't adjusted to it."

"Am I ever glad they didn't sic one of those dogs on us. That would have been curtains."

"If any of those cops were as mean as Clem back there in the Hills, we'd be in for another rough time. Rough."

Soon the train repeated its starting ritual—an abbreviated back and forth jerk—and it was on its way. Wes and I rose from the wrapping paper. It had an exceptional thickness to it and must have come off a gigantic roll. I looked it over carefully and explained, "This paper was probably used to seal the car to ship grain, probably wheat. I saw paper like it at a Sioux Center grain elevator. Basically the car looks like one made to haul autos or farm machinery. That's what all those rods are about up there. But this auto car may have been pressed into hauling grain during the peak of harvesting. Like I said, that's what this paper was for, keeping the grain from getting out through the cracks."

Though highly inquisitive about what was going on outside the car we waited until the train picked up speed and we were certain we had left the city. We appreciated the cops' oversight and were not about to expose ourselves.

When we peered out the open car door we were clearly out of the railroad yards and into the countryside. The Black Hills, which were immediately before us, were marvelous. We shook our heads in disbelief of their beauty.

"It's wonderful to see those hills, and it's been a wonderful vacation to travel among them."

Wes shared the enthusiasm. "I never thought they would be so big and sharp. They should really be called the Black Mountains."

"You know, when we were sitting along the creek in Sioux Center and first talked about this trip, I never thought it would be this good. Never."

"Me neither."

After a moment's thought I modified my thought. "So far, so good. Let's hope our luck keeps on."

The train picked up speed and an excruciatingly loud vibration rang throughout the car. The vibration came with the increase of speed. We ran around the car trying to discover where the noise was coming from. After some wild speculation we learned that a superstructure of rods was bolted to the top of the car. The rods' extended ends were slamming against the steel roof as the train shook and moved.

"This is driving me crazy," Wes shouted as he covered his ears.

"I had a feeling this was a bad car."

"I sure had that bad feeling about the brakeman who put us in here. That bum must have known what kind of a car this is. He must have known."

Without any more loss of time I tore my handkerchief into shreds and wadded them up as earplugs. Wes took two and I put the two remaining ones in my ears. That really helped, though Wes and I could not talk to each other without shouting. We sat down on the floor with our backs against the wall of the box car. We found that comfortable and rode along in ease. The intense noise continued, but with the ear plugs everything seemed okay.

The train made a surprising stop after about an hour. Looking out, we discovered a small town. The engine took on water as it huffed and puffed in a relaxed way. We seized the opportunity to find a more suitable car and bolted through the door, leaving our gear behind. Every freight car was checked but not one was open. So we scampered back to our car as the engineer sounded his warning whistles and jumped in as the train moved out.

I complained, "This is a hell of a situation. Really is."

"It's worse than that," Wes emphasized.

"On the positive side, we got some exercise."

"It's needed if we're going to get in shape for football. We've done some walking, but mostly standing on the this trip. That's not much."

We sat down in our old positions. Wes continued, "You know, there's been so much excitement that we didn't have any supper." He pulled the extension cord from around the broken suitcase, wire that had served so well, and pulled cans of beans and peaches from inside. I, in turn, pulled a couple of spoons from my pocket and with Wes's skill with the can opener we settled back against the side of the box car and had our evening meal.

"This is a bad situation," I grumbled as I unfolded my shelter half and tried to wrap some of the paper around me as a blanket.

Though uncomfortable and upset we settled down to sleep. I thought back to the warm, comfortable and safe Evans dorm and wished we were still there, or in our pup tent camping at Belle Fourche or Deadwood. But that was not the current situation so I gritted my teeth and tried to adjust to the noise. I finally fell asleep but slept fitfully, as the never-ending noise broke through whatever position I took. I awoke several times as I sensed the engine switched onto sidings to let passenger trains pass and also to pick up additional freight cars. All of this activity was accompanied by a great deal of jerking around, pushing and pulling, interspersed with lengthy delays.

I looked up at the darkness above me and could not see the ceiling of the car. Some light came in through the open door. It was reassuring there was a natural world out there. I thought of home, my sister and family, and wondered about the coming football season and whether I would make the team. I had gotten somewhat used to the rough ride and fell back to sleep, deep sleep.

Chapter Ten
Days Nine and Ten: Box Car

Frightened, I jumped up as I felt a tap on my shoulder, but was relieved to see Wes face to face. But it was not the usual pleasant expression of Wes's that I saw, but one of fear. He murmured, "I can't figure out what's happening. The train is not moving. No noise, it's deadly quiet. Can't hear the engine, nothing."

I pulled the plugs from my ears and listened ever so carefully. I couldn't hear a thing and in a frightened voice said, "It's absolutely still. Absolutely!"

We jumped up, saw a beam of light coming through the cracks that framed the closed car door and ran to it. Wes tried to pull the door open and when he failed I lent my weight to pull it open, thinking that surely would do it.

In spite of our best efforts, however, the door did not move, not an inch. We tried again and again without success. The door on the other side of the car had been locked when we entered the car. Though we knew that, we attacked that door with all of our strength. But our strenuous pulling and pushing did not change it. It was as it was. Wes shouted the obvious and devastating fact. "We're locked in!"

Gripped by overwhelming fear, I shouted with equal force, "You're right! We're locked in! We're locked in!"

We ran to the first door and pounded on it furiously, kicked its middle section where we thought the latch was, hoping that someone would hear us or that we might break out. Neither happened. I looked at Wes and though I could hardly see him I noticed a strange worry that I had never seen before. I cried out, "What are we going to do? What are we going to do?"

He shook his head but said nothing.

Pale with fear we dashed around the car, hoping to find an exit. We knew such was unlikely but our panic pressed us to discover the undiscoverable. Despite my terror I recalled the jackknife in my hip pocket . I hurriedly pulled it out, opened it and attacked the heavy wood frame of the door, aiming at the section where I thought it most vulnerable. But the knife was no match for the heavy, hard wood, and efforts to splinter it failed when the blade broke. My fear exploded. "Now that way to escape is gone!" I cursed the knife and threw what remained of it on the floor.

The alarm swept back and forth between us as we recognized our hopeless situation. Wes, though desperate, had not given up completely. He exclaimed, "Let's try the ceiling, the roof. Sometimes there are doors, like trap doors, that are cut in from the roof."

We had seen such on refrigerator cars but none on cars like this one. They would have no purpose. "I don't think you'll find any up there, Wes."

Yet the hopelessness of our situation pushed Wes to make a try. "Maybe. Just maybe." He climbed up and around the steel rods. There was just enough light coming in through the cracks of the door that I could vaguely see him climb around as if he were among the rafters of a house. However, this was not as simple as that. I heard him swear as he hit rods and moved from one end of the car to the other. "Nothing up here. No opening. Nothing!" he shouted and then climbed down. I held him as he jumped to the floor.

I wanted to say, "Good try," like players say in sports, but I felt it was weak.

At our wits' end, we sat down on the floor of the car. I wondered about the folks back home. Though I wished it, I knew they wouldn't send out a call for our rescue. They had not the slightest notion of where we were, that we were stranded and holed up in a boxcar. The secrecy about our trip was really hurting us.

We had been holding back a runaway fear, raw panic. Now it all broke out in a torrent. We broke down and cried and cried.

"We're not only locked in," Wes called out, "we're stranded on some railroad siding way out from where anyone is or where anything is going on. It's just too quiet out there to be anything else."

I simply nodded my head in despair. There was such a side track south of Sioux Center where boxcars were parked, sometimes for several weeks at a time, even longer, until the railroad company had some use for them. I imagined we were in an even more remote place, some place in the western part of the state. We had seen many such places on our way west but never believed they had any future importance for us.

We continued to thrash around the car for upwards to an hour, hoping against hope to find an escape. We stopped crying, but the terror remained. Wes shook his head. "I don't know what else we can do. We have tried everything. We'll just have to wait to see if anybody finds us."

I agreed but felt there was little chance of that, given the apparent remoteness of the location. "Look," I said, "let's make up a card game using the stubs of the tickets we bought to get into the Wind Cave and the parks." I apologized, "Wes, I know it's not much. It won't solve anything, but we have to keep busy."

I continued to explain the game. "Let's order the cards by their numbers. The different colors can make up the suits. We're going to be short on cards, but we can still make up a game, some kind of a game."

Wes was not impressed as he continued thinking about possible ways out of the car, but he listened and I explained, "We have to do something with our time or we'll go crazy."

He nodded his head glumly. "Okay, I'll go along with that."

"Let's just start really simple. I'll put them all in a pile and we can take turns drawing just to see who gets the highest numbers on the stubs. After we do that for a while we can try 'Fish.' I think I have enough cards to play the game. Remember how it goes? We cut the cards and draw to see who has the highest card. That person is then the dealer, giving each player five cards face down. The guy on the dealer's left starts. Since there are only two of us it's easy to know who begins."

I continued explaining the rules. "You have to have a pair or a run of three to discard. The idea is to get rid of all your cards. The player who does that first wins that hand. We keep a record of how many cards the loser had in his hand at the end of each round. Then, of course, the one with the lower score is the winner."

Wes responded, "Well, how in the heck are we going to do all that without enough cards?"

"I'll make all I can. Then let's try it. Let's try to make it work. We have to do something."

Wes said, "Okay."

"Better than sitting here and worrying and worrying. Worrying ourselves crazy."

We played cards for several hours, continually adjusting the rules to accommodate the limited number of cards. Even though we were engrossed in the card game we remained alert for any sound outside the car. Yet there were none excepting the whistling of the wind. The anguish in our souls continued to flare.

"It's really heated up in here," Wes said as he wiped the perspiration from his forehead. Perspiration was also soaking his shirt. I was uncomfortable but had neglected to observe the heat. But as I saw Wes suffering, I too felt the intense heat. I pulled my shirt off and laid it at the wall of the car.

"There's no way to escape this heat."

"And it will get worse."

"And no water."

"This is the third time that thirst has struck us. First time we got water from that highway work crew outside of Chamberlain."

"That was way back when we were hitching to Rapid. That was our first day out."

"And when we were in the middle of the Bad Lands. That was on the first day out too, but was our second encounter with thirst."

"But now we are really in for it. No water and no way of getting any."

"We have the peaches. They'll help."

"But they aren't water."

Thinking that it was early afternoon Wes opened a can of spaghetti, then changed his mind. "Let's start with peaches."

We passed them back and forth, then turned to the spaghetti. Neither of us mentioned it, but we were thankful to Wes's father for the food, especially the peaches.

We returned to sitting with our backs to the wall. We sat there in a stupor, trying to handle the heat, but the heat wouldn't be handled. Wes had pulled his shirt off and I used my shirt as a washcloth, wiping my face and shoulders.

Feeling the heat was getting to be too much, I stripped down to my boxer shorts and said, "I've got a new game." I pulled four buttons off my shirt and gave Wes two. "Let's toss to win using that hole in the floor. It's not too deep, but deep enough."

We were well adapted to the darkness and played the game slowly and with determination. Sweat rolled off our faces and dropped to the floor. Maybe an hour passed and we were as exhausted as if we had finished a set of tennis. We retreated to the wall of the car and leaned back. The silence was so complete we could hear each other's breathing.

"My mouth is beginning to feel like it did when we were in the bottom of the Bad Lands without any water and without a ride."

"That was bad, even worse than when we were just outside of Chamberlain in the heat of the afternoon and couldn't get a ride."

"Remember we were able to get water from that highway work crew. That was a surly group."

"At least we got some. . . . Here there's no such chance."

"Here we don't have any," Wes muttered. "We do have the syrup in the peaches, and I think we have a few cans of tomatoes. All that should help, but we've got to go slow on them."

"We may be here for a long time. Let's just have one of them tonight. No more. You know, either peaches or tomatoes."

My apprehension moved out of control. I screamed, "God! I wish somebody would find us! I can't face the horrible thought of a slow death." I broke out in a fervent prayer asking the Lord to save us, to forgive my sins and help us find the way home. Tears ran down my cheeks and as I ended my prayer I broke down and cried and cried.

Wes joined in and after a period of praying and crying we returned to our immediate situation. Wes, with conviction, said, "Someone will come soon. They've got to! I know it!"

We waited for an encouraging sign but none came, and we continued to sit on the floor of the car. Finally we lay down and fell asleep.

We awoke early in the evening. We could see the intensity of the light coming through the cracks of the door had diminished. A chill of horror covered us as we confessed a perishing hope of being found. Our prayers had done no good. None. Not only had help failed to come but I, and I thought Wes too, continued our awful desperation.

I had prayed to Jesus and to the Lord. I had Catholic friends who recommended the Virgin Mary, so I tried her and recalled all the sins I could, feeling that a confession might be traded for freedom. Many things came to my guilty mind and I blurted them out: stealing fruit from the neighbors' fruit trees, fishing out of season, shooting pigeons off a neighbor's roof, swimming in the fish hatchery, keeping collector stamps off of selection sheets without paying, keeping Sunday school coins instead of putting them in the collection plate and knocking bulbs from street lights with rocks. I desperately hoped that such an array of admissions would surely persuade the good Mother to do something miraculous for us, specifically to open the box car door.

But the Virgin Mary didn't do any more for us than Jesus and the Lord. I couldn't understand it. I believed I was a good person; not the best, because I knew I had many flaws, but not so many that I deserved being locked up in a box car, one that was isolated and forlorn.

"Looks like our jig is up," I complained. "We've been in here a day now. No one has come by and it doesn't look like anybody will."

Wes, with a note of resignation, added, "I'll open a can of beans and one of peaches. Let's see what happens after that. Maybe, just maybe, someone will wander by. I sure as God hope so." Wes did not take his eyes off the floor of the car as he spoke. He looked up for a moment and I caught his eyes, and we looked at each other in desperation, hoping to pick up encouragement from each other, knowing that none was forthcoming. Our plight had worsened, not improved.

A moment later we thought we heard someone, some movement outside. We jumped up, ran to the door and pounded on it furiously at the same time shouting like mad. We stopped after a minute or two to learn whether anyone had heard us. We listened closely, but heard nothing except the wind blowing. Though useless, we repeated our pounding and shouting, hoping there would be a person to hear us. We decided that there was no one. Hence, no response. I hung my hands by my sides in despair and Wes shook his head.

I had a hard time saying it, but I did. "Looks like we're lost and forgotten."

Wes nodded. After a moment he said, "At least the air has cooled, but that awful grain dust stink hangs on."

"Using the other end of the car as a toilet hasn't helped the stink."

"God, no."

We had put our clothes back on as the temperature chilled. We lay down on our shelter halves and covered ourselves with paper. Wes said, "Thank God for this. The nights are cold here, wherever we are."

I did not answer, as I had nothing more to say. I fell asleep thinking about the grandeur of Mt. Rushmore, Mr. Evans and my sister and family.

My sleep was fitful because I continued to dream about being lost in a desert, fighting sand storms. The dream repeated itself in spite of my efforts to forget it, to put it out of mind. I tried counting to one hundred, thought about making the football team and starring, about being rescued from the box car, but none worked. The awful dream continued to repeat itself.

For some strange reason my dreams finally stopped and I recalled my mother sitting at the kitchen table about two years ago. It was cold outside. She shoveled extra coal into the stove to fight the intense cold. "Carl," she said thoughtfully, and with grave concern, "I'm going to the Yankton hospital next week for an operation."

"Why?" I asked fearfully. "Why?"

"They have to cut me open and take out a tumor."

Frozen by fear I was only able to nod my head.

I continued that line of thought and remembered the actual experience.

We all went to Yankton the following week—my sister Alta and her husband Bill, my brother Elmer, two years older than myself, and I. The hospital was a foreign environment for me— the long hallways, Catholic sisters with unique attire, the hurrying of nurses and the smell. The smell was especially penetrating and reminded me of our chicken coop after spraying it with disinfectant. There weren't any lice here but I imagined they kept the place especially clean to guard against such problems.

My mother was placed on a cart and wheeled to the operating room where she remained about three or four hours. My brother-in-law Bill was allowed to observe the operation and returned with vivid details, including the removal of a tumor about the size of a grapefruit. How such could grow inside my mother baffled me.

We returned home shortly thereafter, as my mother was still under anesthesia. Why no one remained with her bothered me, but I said nothing. The return home was about a forty-mile drive. Bill and Alta dropped Elmer and me off at Sioux Center en route to their farm. Without mother, Elmer and I occupied the house. It was lonesome and scary.

I shifted to our immediate problem and prayed to her. "I know you're gone, gone someplace up there. We need your help so badly. Please help us. Please help us."

After my prayer I recalled having returned to school the next day in a quandary, wondering about my mother, feeling she would not make it out of the hospital. I got a phone call the second evening I was home from the hospital asking me to come, as my mother was lonesome and afraid. I was only thirteen and inexperienced, but I said I would come.

I caught a passenger train the next morning and reached the hospital about noon. Though apprehensive and ridden with fear,

I visited with my mother until late afternoon. Then I had to find a place to stay. There were no more trains home. I didn't get any help from the hospital people. So I went out on the street and solicited a place to stay door to door. Finally after an hour's search, which was made miserable by flurries of snow, I found a place that would give me room and board for two nights. No more, the lady said. "We're not accustomed to doing this but we'll help you."

The charge had to be negotiated because I didn't have as much as the lady asked, $4.00 a day. Finally we agreed on $3.50, $7.00 total. That gave me enough money to catch the train back home. That was all the money I had.

It was a nice home, not a rooming house, but I was uncomfortable. It was the home of upper class people, not one that took in roomers. The woman took me because of my sad plight. Dinner was served in a dining room with linen tablecloth and napkins, sterling silver dinnerware, real china plates and sparkling glasses for water or milk. A brilliant chandelier hung over our heads, and intellectual talk took place. There were three boys in the picture, one my age and two older. They joined their parents in talk that was out of my realm—city politics and world affairs. I decided the father was an attorney.

Though I got acquainted with the boy my age, Albert, and liked him, the whole situation was unfamiliar to me. That and worry about Mother made me uneasy.

Visiting with my mother during the following two days was wearing. She was feeling bad, and there wasn't much to talk about. She was afraid of dying, and was looking for support. Besides her saying so, I basically felt that was the case.

After two days my money had run out and I was excruciatingly tired. I told her I would be leaving that afternoon. She pleaded with me to stay but I gently said I had to get back to school. This was hard. Then she made it even harder.

"Would you go to see Mr. Warren?" This was her ex-husband and, before the divorce, my stepfather. "Ask him if he would come and see me. I feel like I am being punished by God for something I did to him. I probably should not have left him."

I hated the man. One of the happiest days of my life was when we moved out of his house and returned to our own. I not only hated him, I was afraid of him. So going to see him on behalf of my mother was over my head and I quietly shook my head and said, "You didn't do any wrong."

I left, saying, "I'll be back this week. I know Alta and Bill are coming Saturday." Feeling guilty but relieved, I caught the train home. I was glad to see my brother. However, we did not talk much. Both of us expected the worst and only shared our common gloom.

The following morning I was called to the superintendent's office and was surprised to see my Uncle Louis and Elmer there. "It's about your mother. She's bad. So we better go and see her," was all that Uncle Louis said. The superintendent nodded, and we were on our way. I wondered how my mother was facing death and if she might not already be dead.

Uncle Louis made a few uneasy remarks. "You boys have been living alone for a week now. Have you done your own cooking? How did you get along?" He was being nice but we only nodded to his questions. Besides, they made me uncomfortable because they made me wonder about where we would live after my mother died.

When we arrived at the hospital, Uncle Louis went to the desk. Elmer and I stood in the background. When he returned to us he said, "She's passed away."

I asked, "Does that mean she's dead?"

He nodded his head.

I sat up in the box car and leaned my back against the wood side wall and looked upwards into the dark and prayed to my mother. "Please, please help us here. Tell me what to do." After a pause I added slowly, "Help me face death. I know it's coming. It's coming." That was all I could say as I cried.

I awoke the following morning exhausted. My mouth was cotton-dry and a demanding thirst plagued me.

Wes rubbed his head as he climbed out from under the paper, asking, "Is this the second or third day we've been in here? The way this place smells from our using the one end of

182

the car as a toilet, it seems like it's the third day." He got up and paced back and forth.

"Second," I replied matter-of-factly. "We'll never get out of this awful place," I wailed as I continued to lie on the floor of the car. I was appalled by the idea we would die, or lose our reason, or both. The prayer to my mother hadn't worked. Indeed, the dream and my recollections following it made me feel worse.

Wes stopped walking, came over, put his hand on my shoulder and poured out his terror. "Carl, it looks like we've had it. If I've done anything bad to you, I am sorry. It just looks bad for us. Just does."

I apologized for encouraging the freight train as a mode of travel. How simple standing along a highway without being picked up was compared to this. Even Clem and the Chief back at Silverton were easy compared to our situation now. We both broke into tears. Not embarrassed, we cried without restraint.

Wes pulled a can of peaches from the suitcase. I could see him because of a beam of light that came through the cracks of the door, carrying a futile, but a ray of hope for our rescue.

Our mood shifted from fear, anxiety and panic to moodiness and depression. Anxiety had left us completely, but an all-encompassing doom of our situation took over. We drank the peach juice by gulps and ate the peaches with relish. In the meantime Wes opened a can of beans and we ate them mechanically, trying to control our despondence.

"Mother, hear me and save me." I repeated this plea over and over again.

We were only able to maintain our wakefulness for a short while before we withdrew under the papers and fell asleep.

We were unable to tell the time when we awoke but, we estimated that it was early afternoon. We acknowledged each other but did not speak—there was nothing left to say. The intense thirst came back and we sat gasping for water. We drank some peach syrup, but my tongue had swollen, my throat was dry and my lips had cracked. I licked my lips but it only made them feel worse. I was breathing through my mouth to avoid the stench of the box car and realized it compounded the dryness and thirst. Painfully I forced myself to breathe through my nose and hoped the stink would fade.

Wes looked at the floor as I was adjusting myself to a more comfortable position. He did not look up and I figured he was dreaming of better times. He erupted from his dreaming and shouted, "The stink is driving me mad! It stinks and it stinks of death."

A sudden jolt hit the car and our panting became worse. It was the backward thrust of an engine as it connected cars about to be pulled. Immediately thereafter we heard voices and footsteps. Still gasping, we sprang to the door, pounding and shouting frantically. But no one answered. The train pulled ahead for a short distance and repeated its backward and forward car-connecting jolt. This was repeated several times. We shouted and pounded on the door again and again. After a lapse we heard voices and began pounding with all of our remaining strength. The voices were immediately outside the door.

A gruff voice called out, "There's someone in there!"

And with that, the door slid back. Two brakemen, mixing consternation with anger, shoved the door completely open and shouted, "What the hell are you doing in there?"

We simply exclaimed, "We've been trying to get out. Been in here for two days."

"It figures. This car and others were dropped off here a couple of days ago. It is being taken back to St. Paul where it will carry a shipment of automobiles someplace."

"Do you have any water?" Wes whispered. "We haven't had any for a long time."

"Sure," one of the brakemen said and he raised a three-gallon bucket. "Try this."

I pulled the cover from the bucket and discovered a dipper covered by water. Wes grasped the handle and drunk his fill by gulps. I followed.

The brakemen were nonchalant, which we appreciated. They did not wail or wonder how we were locked in the car or what doom we had just escaped. Nor did they demand that we fill out a report.

The lead brakeman asked, "Where you headed?"

We volunteered, "Mitchell."

"Well, at least you still know where you want to go, so you're in pretty good shape." He laughed. "We are about a hundred twenty-five miles from there. This little siding is outside Draper. That's about forty miles south of Pierre. But, boys, this train is going to Aberdeen, not Mitchell."

The brakeman pulled his cap down over his head tightly. "Something has gone wrong with your engineer or your compass. We're going north, not east. You can either ride up to Aberdeen and go south some way to Mitchell, or jump off here and see if you can catch a freight directly to Mitchell, but I don't know when that will be."

"How far is it from Aberdeen down to Mitchell?" I asked.

"About a hundred fifty miles," the brakeman surmised.

"How long will it take this train to get to Aberdeen?" I pursued.

"We'll get there about midnight. Not a good time to arrive, but this is not a passenger."

"So, we'll ride the rest of the afternoon and half of the night to a place where we'll be twenty-five to fifty miles further from Mitchell than we are now," I said after some figuring.

The brakeman said, "That's right. Your only advantage is that Aberdeen is a better jumping off place than Draper."

I looked at Wes. He threw his hands up in the air and said, "Let's stay with this train."

We rubbed our heads in consternation, realizing that all of the switching we heard several nights ago didn't get us very far. We cursed the brakeman who had put us aboard this car in Rapid City and assured us that it would deliver us to Mitchell. When we boarded the freight in Rapid City we planned to cover the state from west to east. We now would eventually cover it from west to northeast.

I timidly asked the brakeman for another drink of water. This confusion was more than I could readily absorb and it pushed my basic thirst.

"Sorry," the brakeman said. "Sorry if your plans are messed up." He shifted, adding, "I must get on. If you boys ride on we'll be in Aberdeen about midnight. You can jump out there, sleep in the depot and start south on highway 281 bright and early." He paused and added, "I"m not a conductor but I'll keep an eye out for you."

What a nice man, I thought. We thanked him and he was on his way.

Wes and I looked at each other in dismay but agreement. We sat in the open door and dangled our legs over the edge as the freight pulled out. We continued to dangle our feet out the door as we passed over the Missouri River, passed through Mobridge and by Oahe Lake. Only later did we learn that this small community held huge murals painted by a famous Dakota Indian artist, Oscar Howe. Though weak from our lockup experience we enjoyed riding through huge fields of small grains in the process of being harvested. We continued to sit in the open door as the light became dimmer and dimmer.

Finally I said, "It's getting late. If one of us nods asleep he's sure to fall out of the car. I'm going to get some of that paper and jam the door in a couple of places. Two should do it. Besides, I'll lie down right next to the doorway. With my hand touching the door and ready to hold it we should be okay."

If there was any humor to be found, I found it. "Yeah. I would hate to miss Aberdeen and ride on to St. Paul or Minneapolis, locked in."

Wes chuckled, "We've forgotten to eat!

"Too much going on."

"Eating is a small matter compared to getting out of lockup. A small matter."

We ate our staples of beans and peaches. Riding with the car door open lessened the stink. That was a relief.

Our lockup was over but not over. I continued to feel like I was locked up, and if I escaped that feeling by rational thought, the reprieve lasted only a few minutes and my great fear of being locked up returned. I had jammed the door and lay down dangerously close to it, holding its edge in one of my hands.

I continued to consider the day, and I emphasized, "I just feel greater than great about getting out! Have ever since that door was pulled open. Great. Great."

"I know what you mean. Amen," Wes chimed in.

"We're doing the right thing, exactly, by sitting right in the doorway."

"Our doorway to freedom!"

After a pause I asked Wes, "Do you think the prayers helped get us out?"

He shrugged.

"As hard as I prayed, and I tried everybody, even my dead mother, and the Virgin Mary, Jesus, and the Lord God Over All, but I doubt it."

"Why not?" Wes pressed.

"Well . . . I don't think any of those people put us in and by the same reasoning I don't think they had anything to do with getting us out. No, I don't think so."

"So how do you figure it?"

"Bad luck got us in and good luck got us out. Nothing more complicated than that."

Wes shrugged. "You might be right."

"I feel ashamed of making all that fuss and all that praying."

"Why? We were really in a bad shaped. No hope."

"I know. I know. But I'm still ashamed of all that crying and praying."

"Let it go, Carl, and get some sleep."

We arrived in Aberdeen at midnight, as the brakeman had said. We climbed out of the doorway of the now-hated boxcar and staggered out of the freight yard carrying our luggage. "Any more freight train riding?" Wes asked in jest.

I shook my head saying, "No more!"

We headed for the washroom of the railroad station, where we washed up and changed our clothes. Wes smiled as he pointed to the missing buttons on my shirt. "We really were competitive in that button tossing game."

I laughed. "We better save them. We may want to use them again some time."

"And I hope you've kept those cards. They never worked out for the game of 'Fish' but we tried."

We drank our fill of water and returned to the waiting room and looked around, expecting to be ushered out. But that did not happen. No one was there. We curled up on one of the hard wooden benches and went to sleep with our luggage next to us. But before falling asleep I was more worried that someone would lock us in than throw us out, and I rubbed the sweat of my hands onto my shirt.

Chapter Eleven
Day Eleven: Corn Palace

We awoke the next morning as the sounds of mail wagons on the platform drifted into the room. We nodded at each other, went to the toilet and washed up again. Checking ourselves in the mirrors, we decided we looked good enough to hitchhike. We carried our luggage outside, took a can of beans and spaghetti from a suitcase and sat on a bench and had our breakfast. The sun was out, yet the temperature was pleasantly cool.

"It's wonderful to be outside," I said. "We're not going to spend any time here," I continued, "but let's look around inside the depot. I saw they have things about the city on a bulletin board. We'll at least get a glimpse of the place."

We learned that Aberdeen had a wonderful park, Wylie Park, and Sand Lake National Wildlife Refuge was just outside of town on the James River. There was also a teachers' college, a sister institution of Dan Larson's beloved Black Hills Teachers' College at Spearfish. However, we did not tarry to see any of these things. Instead we found our way to Highway 28 and began to thumb our way south. We were exhausted, but our morale had picked up. Even our lips started to heal and my tongue did not feel heavy anymore.

"God, I am glad to be out here on the road, even without a ride," Wes exclaimed.

I did not answer at first, but felt the same. As I thought about what Wes had said, I expressed my concern. "Wes, I keep sweating, even though we've been out of the box car for a long time, a whole night. And I feel kind of funny, almost dizzy. Do you have anything like that?"

"Hm," Wes answered. "I wasn't going to say anything, but I keep feeling like we're going to get closed in. Doesn't make any difference where we go, like into the toilet of the depot or out in the waiting room. That's why I'm so glad to be out here in the open. I really am afraid of going into another building."

I admitted the same preoccupation and said, "I keep hoping it will go away. It makes me nervous. I hate to keep wiping my hands on my pants or shirt."

"I think it will," Wes assured. "We just have to quit thinking about that box car. That's what's causing it."

I nodded, was not assured, but tried to be positive. "I'm sure glad to be out here on the road too."

A number of cars whizzed by but we did not mind. The fresh air, sunshine and freedom was good enough for us. We didn't need anything more.

Finally, a late model Oldsmobile stopped beside us. A sun-tanned, middle aged man with a sombrero in the fashion of Tex Webster motioned for us to come to his side of the car. His motion carried the authority of a man who was used to wielding it, and did it often and easily. We responded but did not feel imposed upon.

"Boys, how far south are you going?" he asked lazily.

"Mitchell," I said.

He sat back in his seat smiling. "That's about a hundred and fifty miles. I'm just going about eighty miles down the road." He paused and looked us over with a sharp eye. "I guess I can trust you. Where are you from?"

We responded, "Sioux Center."

"And what are you doing out here?"

"Sightseeing. We were out in the Black Hills exploring the area around there."

"What did you enjoy seeing the most?"

"Many, many things. Mt. Rushmore, State Game Lodge, Wind Cave, Sylvan Lake, the whole thing."

"What did you say your names are?"

"Wes and I'm Carl."

We had gone through such questioning many times before. We responded easily and candidly, being sure, however, to leave out our box car lock-in. We didn't want to get into that. It was more than we could talk about.

"Very good, boys," the man answered. "Get in. My name is Walter Thomas." He did not miss a thought as we got in, and he continued, "I own a large farm down the road. Some people call it a ranch, but that sounds too fancy for me. I like farm better. But boys, I wouldn't do anything else, even though farming is tough business. Always plenty of worries."

Though I thought I knew the worries because my relatives often talked about their farming problems, I bluntly asked, "What are they?" That was a mistake.

He blustered on. "Maybe the weather is the biggest worry. Will it be too hot or cold for the crops and farm animals? Will there be enough or too much rain for the crops? Then you have the worry about your machinery. Will it work? If so, for how much longer? Will I have to replace it soon? And if so, where do I get the money?"

Mr. Thomas sighed. "Then you've got prices to worry about, price for hogs, price for cattle, price for chickens and eggs, price for cream, price for corn, price for machinery, and so on. I don't mean to cry, boys, but it's tough, because you're always working on a close margin between what it costs you to produce and what the market will pay."

Mr. Thomas shook his head and shifted his tone. "It's not as bad as I'm making it, because I really like the independent life of a farmer. I set my own schedule, keep my own hours, run my own business, solve my own problems. So it's a good life. I've raised my family out here and they've done well."

He droned on. We were exhausted by our box car incident and fell asleep. We slept for an hour. When we awoke, Mr. Thomas was driving into Huron, which seemed sizeable. When he noticed we were awake he suggested, "It's time for lunch. There's a little hamburger joint just up the road a ways. If you'll agree, I'll stop there."

We nodded our heads and looked forward to something besides beans, spaghetti and peaches.

He stopped at a place called Hamburger House. "This is a great place," Mr. Thomas announced. "They give real service. You can order and be served right in your car." We all ordered giant hamburgers, french fries and Cokes. We offered to pay but Mr. Thomas waved his hand. "The treats are on me," he continued. "Boys, this is the end of the line for me. I'll drive you to the south edge of town so you can make a fresh start from there."

We thanked him for the lunch and the ride and for dropping us off at the south side of town. We jumped out of his shiny Oldsmobile and positioned ourselves on the side of Highway 37. "We're about fifty miles from Mitchell," Wes said with a smile.

I asked Wes anxiously, "Were you relieved that we ate in the car instead of going into that hamburger joint?"

"Well, yes, but I could have gone in there. All in all I think I was less afraid than I was in the railroad depot. Maybe I'm getting better. How about you?" he asked. "I didn't see you wiping your hands on your shirt so much."

"Maybe we are on the road to recovery. It's true. I don't sweat as much and I don't feel as dizzy, but I am still scared."

Wes sat on his suitcase. The wire cord held firmly, and he was safe. "You do the thumbing. I'm really all done in."

Though very tired too, I agreed.

Several semi-trailer trucks ground by. The drivers waved in good spirits but did not stop. Finally a highly polished Studebaker slowed, but passed us. The woman driving was alone, and she scrutinized us closely as she drove by. She slowed even more, finally stopping about twenty yards ahead of us. She sounded her horn. I couldn't figure out what she meant by that but I didn't want to miss a ride so I ran the distance, stopped by her window ready to answer any questions.

She began slowly, showing some nervousness. "Are you boys looking for a ride?"

"Yes, we are."

"Why are you out here? And why isn't that fellow back there not up here? Why is he sitting back there on the suitcase?"

I answered these questions. She followed with, "Please have that other fellow come up here, but before you do tell me why you have so much luggage."

"We've been to the Black Hills camping, took our own tent."

She was satisfied but challenged, "If you were in the Black Hills, what are you doing coming down this road? You ought to be on Highway 90 coming east."

Her suspicions prompted me to tell her about being pulled by a freight in the wrong direction while asleep. I skipped the box car story. It was too complicated and continued to be too painful to go over.

She seemed satisfied and turned to Wes, who had joined us. She asked him essentially the same questions that she had asked me and got the same answers. She was satisfied with that and offered, "I'm Miss Wayman, County Superintendent of Schools. I want to help you. But can I trust you?"

We were desperate for a ride and made the very best plea for our trustworthiness. She kept a close critical eye on us as we made our case. She was convinced, nodded her head sharply and directed us to get our luggage.

Miss Wayman was a slight woman in her early forties. She was pretty and her hair, which was beginning to gray, had a smart upturn sweep on the sides and back of her head. Its ends were in a knot supported by combs at the top of her head. Her eyes were brown, not light, but black-like, and carried an intenseness. Her brow was slightly wrinkled and she frowned occasionally as she spoke. Overall I got the impression that she was a determined, no-nonsense woman.

That she was in charge became evident when she continued, "In Dawson County, which is my responsibility, I am trying to change the high dropout rate among teenagers. So I want to know from you, Wes and Carl, are you going back to school in the next week?"

Before we could answer she challenged, "Are you?"

She was pleased with our answer but continued her challenge. "Are you spending real time on your course work? Are you studying hard?"

Again we replied positively.

She nodded her head, asking. "And behaving in the classroom?" This question had an emphasis beyond the others. "Really being responsible and behaving?"

We nodded almost meekly as Miss Wayman bore down. "Are you keeping active?" she pursued. "Out for athletics, trying to make one team or another?"

"Yes," we answered. "We are going out for football in just a week."

She seemed satisfied, relaxed a bit at the steering wheel but questioned us further. "Now, what are your career choices? Have you given any serious thought to that?"

I did less well on that. "I'm not sure. I'd like to be a geologist, but my math isn't very good. So I probably will have to try something else, but I don't know what. Maybe teaching and coaching."

Wes was more clear. "I'd like to be a scientist. I think I can make it. But it's a long, hard road."

"Right," Miss Wayman agreed. "You might as well get started in on it and keep your grades up as high as you can.'"

Wes nodded and I figured what she said applied to me too. We seemed to have hit a plateau with Miss Wayman. We enjoyed her challenge. We were especially pleased that she pushed the Studebaker along at sixty-five miles an hour. That meant we would be in Mitchell soon.

I asked, "We've heard a lot about the Corn Palace. Is it really worth seeing?"

Miss Wayman did not back away from the question and she gave us a firm, public relations answer. "The outside is always beautiful. In fact, it's unusually beautiful and clearly different from anything you'll ever see. The inside depends on what exhibits are showing. Sometimes those exhibits are great—for example, art exhibits. Sometimes there's nothing on display, as they may be setting up for a Dakota Wesleyan University basketball game. So it all depends."

She shrugged her shoulders, saying, "I don't know what's there now. But I'll drop you right in front of the place, if you like. Walk around the building several times, look at it from all sides."

We had gotten to like Miss Wayman during our short trip. We appreciated her taking a risk on us. It was not something a woman in her circumstance would ordinarily do. Maybe our sentiment about her was heightened because we were still reeling from the box car experience, but whatever the cause, we felt she was great and hated to leave her. We did, nevertheless, pulling our luggage out after us. She drove away from the curb, waving. We had thanked her but felt it was not enough and wished we could have done more.

After putting our luggage down, we stood in amazement as we viewed the beauty of the murals made with different colored corn, grains and grasses. What we saw immediately was the state seal showing a grain binder running through a field of rich farm land. Crowded onto the scene was a miner panning gold, a smoke stack of a factory and a mighty buffalo. All of these blended together, though the colors were in sharp contrast. After absorbing the beauty of one side of the building, we persuaded an attendant to accept our luggage for safekeeping and walked around to the other sides of the building.

First we saw a mural of Indians and whites, including military men, next to what appeared to be a peace-making table. The Indians and whites were shaking hands and showing good will. We walked to another side of the Corn Palace and saw a one-room country schoolhouse on a flat prairie with children playing in the school yard and a teacher standing in the background. We were amazed that pictures of people, as in the previous mural, could be created by ears of corn, grains and grasses.

Walking to the third side of the building we saw another impressive mural. This one showed a cowboy rounding up a herd of cattle. They were cast in a large acreage. A blue sky and sun stood out overhead. We walked back and forth as we took in the full scope of the picture. We did not speak but shook our heads in amazement.

We crossed the street to get a long view of the murals and started around the building again. We were even more impressed on our second trip around. Finally, we entered the building, smiling at the attendant holding our luggage. We hoped she would not ask us to pick it up. She didn't.

We did not expect to see murals on the inside as well, but were surprised. They were there too. We moved slowly, from wall to wall. We saw a steamboat on the mighty Missouri River, huge cattle drives, educational institutions, none of which we recognized excepting Old Main at the University of South

Dakota. We had seen photos of it in the *Yankton Daily* that was delivered to Sioux Center.

Plaques on the wall told of the Corn Palace being about a hundred years old, and that redecorating was done every year and on new themes. A festival of entertainment, displays and exhibits was scheduled but that was to take place several weeks later, when we would be in school.

The attendant not only returned our luggage with a smile, but told us of a park nearby in which we could camp. It was mid-afternoon. We were tired. A grocery store appeared en route to the park. We entered, purchased a couple of steaks, bread, rolls and milk for breakfast. As we still had sufficient funds for shopping, we disregarded the cost.

We walked on, found the park and set up our tent on a site near the showers and toilets. Other campers were on the grounds. Because we were so tired, we did not shower but built our fire, roasted our steaks and ate with relish. The steak provided the nourishment we needed after our torturous experience in the box car. In addition to the steak and bread, Wes opened a can of spaghetti and we passed it back and forth between us, each using his own spoon. Water from a nearby fountain quenched our never-ending thirst.

I remarked, "We've mentioned her often, but Miss Walsh would frown severely at our style." We were happy, and after laughing about Miss Walsh's etiquette lessons, we dropped the subject. Around eight o'clock we climbed into the tent, falling asleep without any conversation.

Chapter Twelve
Day Twelve: Going Home in Style

The following morning we were awakened by the noise of campers who were leaving. Their tents were pulled down, packed on top of their cars and then they departed.

We had rolls and milk, then pulled down our tent, folding it with the feeling of "getting on with it." We did not speak but I had a great sense of freedom and I felt Wes did too. We were exceptionally happy to be out of the box car and on our way home. Good rides, nice people, good food, great sightseeing and exciting camping—it was all coming together. I consciously left out the hot cinder shower on our first freight ride and the snake scare in the sand car, the jail experience and the box car lockup.

"Let's take a rest, just a little one before we get on the road," I encouraged. "Let's just take a few minutes."

We sat down and Wes asked, "How much money do you have?"

"About seven dollars," I answered.

"Would you count it to be sure?"

I pulled a handkerchief from my pocket, untied it and counted my money. "Seven dollars and twenty cents," I answered. "And that's exact."

Wes continued, "You know, I'm really tired. Worn out." His voice had surprisingly little energy.

"I know what you mean. I know what you mean. I'm beat too. Just drained. I don't know if I can really make it today, but we're getting so close to home we've got to keep moving." I shifted a bit. "Do you want to stay on? This is a great park. We can just stay here and rest for a couple of days. By the way, are you still afraid of being closed in?"

"You've asked me a lot of questions. This is a good spot, but I don't want to stay any longer. I want to go home. Now, on the fear of being closed or locked in, it's still with me. I was even afraid of getting into the tent last night, and you know it doesn't even have a front flap on it. No door. But I know it will go away. I'll be all right. It will just take time. How about you?"

"I'm not dizzy any more, but my hands still sweat, maybe less than yesterday, but they still sweat all the time."

"What do you think of catching the train home? I don't mean a freight. I mean a passenger." Tiredness was clearly in his voice. "Two days of worry and thirst is hard to shake off. It's still with me. I'd just like to put worry aside and the hassle of hitchhiking, and the danger of catching a freight. Instead I'd like to ride a passenger."

"What do you think it will cost?" I asked, hoping seven dollars and twenty cents would cover it.

"We can find out. The depot is only a mile or so from here. Sioux Center is only fifty miles from Mitchell. We probably can get a ticket for about a dollar and a half. Maybe a little more."

I, too, was weary to the core, so I agreed. "Let's do it."

We walked to the depot with a pace faster than our aching bodies wanted to travel, but we pushed ahead. The prospect of riding a passenger train spurred us on.

A new kind of excitement grabbed us as we entered the depot, one of going home. We had had the excitement of riding freight trains, capturing a snake, seeing the Bad Lands and the Black Hills, camping out and staying in Mr. Evans' dormitory, meeting a variety of people along the way, fighting the Chief and Officer James, and the depression of the boxcar lockup, but the excitement of going home was special. It had a mellow tone to it, one of seeing our loved ones, one of settling down, one of returning to school and being safe. Given all of that, we prayed the train fare would be within our means.

I approached the agent at the ticket counter, not to inquire about the next freight arrival, but when the next passenger for Sioux Center was due and the fare.

"Where to, son?" the agent asked.

I proudly said, "Sioux Center."

"There's a flyer due at ten o'clock. That's about forty minutes from now. The fare is one seventy-five."

"One seventy-five?" I repeated, just to be sure.

"That's right," the agent responded. "May I sell you two? One for you and one for your friend?" Though the agent responded to my smile he had no idea of the joy that I felt.

Wes called out, "Yes, two."

I pulled my handkerchief from my pocket, undid the knot and drew two dollars from it, giving it to the agent. Wes was going through the same procedure. As I got my change, Wes gave the agent the exact amount.

With the remaining quarter back in my pocket, we clasped our tickets tightly in our fists and sat waiting for the train. I never felt better in my life.

We never experienced a longer forty-minute wait, excepting those many forty minutes in the box car. Even the waits while hitchhiking seemed short in comparison. Finally we heard a familiar engine noise, including the screeching of brakes, hissing of steam and whistle blowing. At the same time the agent called out, "All aboard for passenger south to Parkston, Tripp, Sioux Center, Yankton and beyond!"

We bolted from the bench, grabbed our luggage and quickly moved out onto the platform. We were self-conscious, ill at ease, to be boarding a passenger train. We were used to scurrying around to find an open box car. We walked slowly, trying to appear at ease and as if we did this every day.

The conductor placed a little a step affair, a table-like step, that we stepped on before we ascended up the stairs to the passenger car. We dragged our luggage with us as if it was the finest luggage money could buy and threw it onto a rack that was above the seat below. The Gladstone, though beaten up, stood there proudly with its two straps buckled tightly. The plastic suitcase, which had been broken when thrown from the petroleum freight car when we arrived in Mitchell about twelve days before, also rested proudly on the holding rack and the cord of wire held it at attention. During our travels that suitcase had been disheartening to see, it was so beaten up. But today as I looked it over, including the extension cord, I felt a keen sense of pride in its stature.

We seated ourselves on a double seat that had another double seat facing it. The upholstery was dark red velvet. We decided it needed to be that to take the wear the passengers gave it. As we sat down, the conductor yelled, "Last call! All aboard!" He picked up his little stair-step and boarded the stairs. The train whistled. We were excited and ready to go but were surprised there was no jerking back and forth like that of a freight. Instead it began with a smooth glide, slowly at first, then it picked up speed. Soon the clickety clacking of the wheels on the track told us the train had reached its top speed.

I put my head back against the seat, put my feet in the seat across from us and said, "Wes, there will be no soot and sparks to fight on this one!"

He laughed and added, "And no fear of falling off!"

We watched the countryside roll by as the train sped forth. I asked, "What did you like best about the trip?"

Wes slapped his thigh. "It was getting out of that box car."

"What else?" I asked.

"Oh, a lot of things. You know, them all. And for you?" he countered.

"I'd say the same."

We passed through Parkston and Tripp. Our emotions rose higher and higher as we went through each town. Tripp was especially important because Sioux Center was next in line, excepting Kaylor. I figured we were about fifteen to twenty miles from home. Though actually short, I felt the time would never pass.

Finally the conductor came through the car announcing, "All passengers for Sioux Center be ready to get off at the next stop!" He also took our tickets, which I was worried about, feeling that he might forget.

We rose and pulled our luggage from the rack above. Wes finally acknowledged, "You know, this suitcase has actually gotten light. I wonder if there's anything left in there."

The train finally came to a stop as the conductor yelled, "Sioux Center! All out for Sioux Center."

We stepped off the train. Our pride was high to be reentering Sioux Center on a passenger. We glanced toward the platform and were surprised to see Shorty Hertz.

He looked at us with suspicion as we walked by him and demanded, "Where have you been?"

He was in his usual gruff style, but we had dealt with tougher officers than him. So we casually said, "Traveling," and walked on.

www.ingramcontent.com/pod-product-compliance
Lightning Source LLC
Chambersburg PA
CBHW030434290526
45786CB00001B/281